THE 250 QUESTIONS

YOU SHOULD ASK TO

AVOID FORECLOSURE

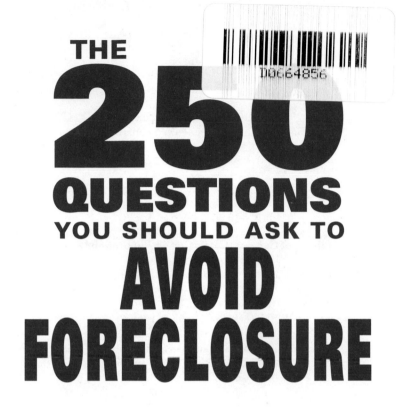

Lita Epstein, M.B.A.

BUSINESS

Avon, Massachusetts

Published by Adams Business
An imprint of Adams Media, an F+W Publications Company
57 Littlefield Street
Avon, MA 02322
www.adamsmedia.com

ISBN-10: 1-59869-511-8
ISBN-13: 978-1-59869-511-3

Library of Congress Cataloging-in-Publication Data
Epstein, Lita.
The 250 questions you should ask to avoid foreclosure /
Lita Epstein.
p. cm.
ISBN-13: 978-1-59869-511-3 (pbk.)
ISBN-10: 1-59869-511-8 (pbk.)
1. Foreclosure—United States—Popular works. I. Title.
II. Title: Two hundred fifty questions you should ask to
avoid foreclosure.
KF697.F6E67 2007
346.7304'364—dc22
2007010761

Printed in Canada.
J I H G F E D C B A

This publication is designed to provide accurate and authoritative information
with regard to the subject matter covered. It is sold with the understanding that
the publisher is not engaged in rendering legal, accounting, or other professional
advice. If legal advice or other expert assistance is required, the services of a com-
petent professional person should be sought.
  —From a *Declaration of Principles* jointly adopted by a Committee of the
American Bar Association and a Committee of Publishers and Associations

Many of the designations used by manufacturers and sellers to distinguish their
product are claimed as trademarks. Where those designations appear in this book
and Adams Media was aware of a trademark claim, the designations have been
printed with initial capital letters.

This book is available at quantity discounts for bulk purchases.
For information, please call 1-800-289-0963.

CONTENTS

INTRODUCTION

Most homeowners who face foreclosure on their property experienced an unexpected job loss or a severe medical emergency. However, other actions, especially the type of loan you choose, can also send you into dangerous financial territory.

If you take a riskier loan, on which you pay very little, if any, of the principal, you could end up facing foreclosure, especially if the interest rate on that loan is variable, which means it can go up yearly as interest rates increase. As your monthly payments get higher and higher, eventually you will not be able to afford that loan.

Another type of risky mortgage allows borrowers to pay less than the interest due as well as nothing on the principal of the loan. With these types of loans you could end up owing more than the house is worth. In order to sell that home, you must come up with cash at closing.

Whatever the reason you are facing foreclosure, all is not lost. You may still be able to save your house by negotiating new terms with your lender or possibly filing bankruptcy. In this book I discuss your options for saving your home and avoiding foreclosure. Whatever you choose to do, don't try to do it on your own. Seek the advice of housing counselors, credit counselors, your attorney, or your accountant. In many situations you may even be able to get help free or at very low cost. I'll point you to some good free resources for help throughout the book.

You will have to work hard to avoid foreclosure, but it is possible for many people to do so, so don't give up hope. Good luck in finding a way to keep your home.

Chapter 1

REVIEWING MORTGAGE BASICS

I n this chapter, I review the basics of the documents you sign when closing on a home mortgage and how they impact your ownership rights, as well as the rights of the financial institution that is loaning you the funds to buy that home.

Question 1: What is a mortgage?

You may not realize this, but a mortgage is a type of loan. In this situation the loan is used to purchase property, and the property being purchased is used as a guarantee for the loan amount. This guarantee then becomes a lien against the property.

After you sign all the papers at closing, the lien is recorded in public records, most likely at your county courthouse. You can't sell your home to someone else until you pay the debt and release the lien. When you close on the sale of your home, these two tasks are taken care of by the closing attorney. Even though you have a mortgage and can't take certain actions until that mortgage is paid off, you still have full title to the property. The lien against the mortgage does give the lender the right to sell the secured property to recover funds if you do not make payments on the debt.

When you apply for a mortgage you can consider several different types of loans, including fixed-rate mortgages, balloon mortgages, adjustable rate mortgages, and interest-only mortgages:

- Fixed-rate mortgages are mortgages for which the interest rate is set when you take the loan, and it remains the same throughout the life of the loan.
- Balloon mortgages are mortgages in which you agree to pay a set interest rate on the loan for a specific period of time. At the end of that period the total amount of the mortgage is due.
- Adjustable rate mortgages, also known as ARMs, are mortgages for which the interest rate changes periodically. When you take this type of loan, the interest rate is pegged to some standard rate, such as a certain percentage above the prime rate.
- Interest-only mortgages are mortgages in which you only pay the interest portion of the loan; your payment does not include any of the principal amount due on the mortgage. The danger with this type of mortgage is that if the value of your house falls below what you paid for it, you will have to come up with extra cash when you sell your home in order to satisfy the lien.

Question 2: **What is a deed of trust?**

In about half the states, a deed of trust is used instead of a mortgage, but just like a mortgage, the deed of trust is recorded in public records to tell everyone that there is a lien on your property.

The deed of trust actually involves three parties. As the homeowner who has taken out the loan, you are the trustor; the financial institution that provides the money for the loan is called the beneficiary; and a neutral third party is the trustee. The trustee is someone who temporarily holds title (but not full title) until the lien is paid.

The deed of trust is canceled when you finish paying the loan. Until that time, the trustee holds the power to foreclose on the debt if you don't make your payments. When a deed of trust is used rather than a mortgage, the trustee can foreclose on the loan without having to go to court. It is easier and faster to foreclose on a home secured by a deed of trust than by a mortgage.

Question 3: **What is a grant deed?**

The grant deed is the document that actually transfers the ownership title to a real estate property from one party, who is known as the grantor, to another party, who is known as the grantee.

The grant deed must describe the property by legal description of boundaries and/or parcel numbers. All people who are involved in the transfer of the property must sign the grant deed, which must be acknowledged before a notary public.

The transfer of ownership of the property is completed when the grant deed is recorded with the County Recorder or Recorder of Deeds. The grant deed warrants that the grantor actually owned the title to the property and that it is not encumbered in any way unless stated in the grant deed.

Question 4: **What is a warranty deed?**

When you close on a piece of property, the most common type of deed you will see is a warranty deed, in which the grantor (seller) guarantees that he or she holds clear title to the real estate property being sold and has a right to sell it to you. In this type of deed the guarantee is not limited to the time the grantor owned the property. The guarantee extends back in time to the property's origins of ownership.

When you do get a warranty deed it should include these statements:

- There are no hidden liens or encumbrances on the property, which means you should not find out about any debts or other holds on the property other than those that you see in public records.
- The grantor declares that he or she owns the property and has the right to sell it to you.
- The grantor guarantees that if the title ever fails, he or she will compensate you as the grantee (new property owner) for any losses incurred defending your title to the property. However, this guarantee might not mean much if the grantor is dead or unable to follow through with his or her promise by the time title problems arise.

You should hire an attorney who specializes in real estate law to perform a title search for you. As an extra precaution you can purchase title insurance, which can protect you from losses that could occur if problems are discovered at a later time.

Question 5: **What is a loan broker?**

A loan broker is a financial professional who does not work for one particular lender, but instead seeks to find you the best rate for the type of mortgage you want from numerous potential lenders. A good loan broker will help you sort through the pros and cons of various loan products available and help you determine which product best meets your needs and individual circumstances. When you work with a loan broker you will have the greatest number of options and terms available.

Question 6: **What is a lender?**

Any institution or individual who loans you money can be considered a lender. The most common type of lender in the mortgage business is a commercial lender, which is usually a banking institution, but can sometimes be a private financial group.

When you use this type of lender you will get an offer for a loan with certain terms that include the interest rate you will be charged and the length of the loan.

If you are considering a balloon loan, you may end up dealing with a hard money lender, which is a lender that specializes in short-term loans that are backed primarily with real estate as collateral. A hard money lender generally offers worse rates than a traditional bank institution, but offers more flexible terms and is more willing to back riskier loan situations.

If you belong to a community credit union, you may find lower loan rates than you can find through a commercial bank. These mutual organizations are nonprofit, and so are able to give higher rates on savings and lower rates on loans.

Another source for people with very low credit scores is a lender of last resort. These are private institutions that loan to people who are considered to be at extremely high risk of default. Your terms for this type of loan will include exorbitant interest rates.

Question 7: **What is a promissory note?**

A promissory note is often used in conjunction with a mortgage. This note is a contract that details the terms of the repayment of the property loan. The note will include the principal amount, the interest rate, and the maturity date (the date by which you must pay the principal in full). The party who promises to pay is called the maker, and the party he or she will pay is called the payee.

In addition to the loan terms, you will likely see provisions concerning the rights of the payee to collect its money in the case of a default. This process usually includes the foreclosure of the maker's interest in the property. When a promissory note is used in conjunction with a mortgage, it is written as a negotiable instrument governed by Article 3 of the Uniform Commercial Code. A negotiable promissory note can be sold to a third party, who then has the rights of the payee to collect on the debt.

Question 8: **What is an institutional lender?**

Any institution that lends money for an interest fee and whose loans are regulated by law, such as a commercial bank, savings bank, a life insurance company, or a savings and loan association, is called an institutional lender. Pension and trust funds can also fit under the umbrella as an institutional lender.

An institutional lender must be an organization that lends money received from its depositors. This differs from a private lender, who lends his or her own money.

Question 9: **What is a private lender?**

A private lender is someone who lends you money to buy real estate from his or her private funds. Your rates will be higher, but your terms for the loan may be better.

The owner of the property can even become a private lender and offer you a deal in which he or she finances the deal with owner financing. The biggest advantage of private lending is the minimal approval process and the speed with which you can get an answer. You also don't have to pay a loan origination fee or "points."

You don't have any limit to the number of mortgages you can get from private lenders, and mortgages through private lenders don't show up on your credit report. But, remember you must expect to pay a higher interest rate for a mortgage from a private lender than you would for one from an institutional lender.

Question 10: **What is a conventional loan?**

Loans that are secured by government-sponsored entities (GSEs), such as Fannie Mae or Freddie Mac, are called conventional loans. These types of loans can be used to purchase or refinance single-family homes and multifamily homes up to homes for four families.

Each year Fannie Mae and Freddie Mac set a limit for mortgage loans, which was $417,000 in 2006 for a single-family home. The limit is reviewed annually and changed, if necessary, to reflect the average price for a single-family home. Conventional loan limits in 2006 for first mortgages on homes larger than single family were $533,850 for two-family homes; $645,300 for three-family homes; and $801,950 for four-family homes. If the home loan was for property in Alaska, Hawaii, Guam, or the U.S. Virgin Islands, the original loan amount could be 50 percent higher for the first mortgage.

Conventional loans for second mortgages are also available through GSEs. The maximum conventional loan for a second mortgage was $208,500, but if the home was in Alaska, Hawaii, Guam, or the U.S. Virgin Islands, the maximum was $312,750.

If you are looking for a loan higher than these amounts, you can get a jumbo loan. These loans are not funded by the GSEs and usually carry higher interest rates, as well as additional underwriting requirements, which means you've got to jump through more hoops to qualify for the loan.

Question 11: What is an FHA loan?

You can buy a house with less money down if you buy a home using a Federal Housing Administration (FHA) loan. These government loans are geared primarily to first-time home buyers or to buyers who don't have enough money to put down on a home to qualify for a conventional loan. The FHA allows you to buy a home with as little as 3 percent down, while you must put 5 percent down for a conventional loan.

In actuality the FHA does not make home loans, but instead insures the loans that a bank makes. If you default on your payments, the lending institution is paid from an insurance fund established by the FHA. In most cases, to qualify for an FHA loan you must have a good credit history and sufficient income. This usually means that your total monthly housing costs cannot exceed 29 percent of your gross monthly income. These housing costs include principal, interest, property taxes, and insurance, often called your PITI.

You can calculate your PITI allowed under an FHA loan by multiplying your gross monthly income times 29 percent. For example, if your gross monthly income is $4,000, multiply that times .29 and you get $1,160.

Question 12: **What is a DVA loan?**

A DVA loan is a loan program for veterans that gives them a way to buy homes without providing a down payment as long as the purchase price is not more than the reasonable value of the property, which is determined by the Veterans Administration. These loans are fixed-interest-rate loans that are competitive with conventional mortgage rates.

Most DVA loans are assumable, but the person who wants to assume a DVA loan must prove his or her creditworthiness. If you are a veteran and you permit your DVA loan to be assumed, you cannot apply for another DVA loan until the first loan is paid off.

If someone holds a DVA loan and is experiencing temporary financial difficulty, the VA will usually be more lenient than would a commercial or private lender. You can find out more about DVA loans at the Web site for the Veterans Administration (*www.homeloans.va.gov*).

Question 13: **What is the difference between a first, second, and third mortgage or loan?**

When you initially buy a home, the mortgage or loan that you arrange is called the first mortgage or senior mortgage. The mortgage holder in this case will have first rights to any money from the sale of the property, whether you sell the property or the debt is foreclosed on for nonpayment of the debt.

If you decide to borrow additional money over and above your initial mortgage, the next level of debt is called a second mortgage. This is commonly the case with an equity line of credit. In this case the lender is subordinate to the first mortgage lender, which means if you sell the property or the property is foreclosed on, the second mortgage lender will only get paid with funds left after the first mortgage lender is paid off.

If you take a third loan on the property, it will become subordinate to both the first and second mortgage. In this case, the lender on the third mortgage or loan will only get paid after the first and second mortgage lenders are paid.

Question 14: **What is private mortgage insurance?**

Any time you purchase a home with less than 20 percent down, a lender likely will require you to get private mortgage insurance (PMI). This insurance is not paid to you if you are not able to make your payments. It is paid to the lending institution if you default on your loan agreement.

Don't confuse PMI with mortgage life insurance. PMI does not make your mortgage payments if you are unable to make the payments because of illness or death. You will need to pay a certain amount each month to have PMI insurance, but once the value of your home goes up enough that you have at least 20 percent equity in the home, you may be able to stop paying PMI.

The primary purpose of PMI is to allow you to buy a home with a lower down payment. For instance, if you wanted to buy a $300,000 home but only had $15,000 (5 percent) to put down, you could buy the home with PMI. Without PMI you would need 20 percent down on the same home, or $60,000.

Chapter 2

UNDERSTANDING FORECLOSURE BASICS

No one wants to think about the possibility of losing his or her home, but it can happen if you run into financial difficulty and can't pay the mortgage. In this chapter, I review the basics of foreclosure, how it works, and what you can expect if you're not able to pay the mortgage.

Question 15: **What is foreclosure?**

Foreclosure is the means by which your lender can legally repossess (take ownership) of your home from you if you aren't living up to your end of the bargain—making your payments to the lender. Once the lender forecloses on your home, you must move out of the home or you will be evicted.

In addition to losing your home, you could even owe the lender more money. That happens if the value of your home is less than the amount you owe on your mortgage loan.

There are two possible types of foreclosures. One type is called a judicial foreclosure. The second is called a non-judicial foreclosure. I explain these two procedures in greater detail later in this chapter. In either case, your property would likely be auctioned to the highest bidder by the county sheriff or some other officer of the court. Often the lender bids on the house at the auction, at the price of the debt owed. If no other buyer bids higher, the bank wins the property.

Question 16: **What is pre-foreclosure?**

Pre-foreclosure is the time period between the day you get a notice that the lender has filed a foreclosure lawsuit or a Notice of Default in the official public records and the actual date the property will be sold at a public foreclosure auction or trustee's sale.

When you get the notice, you still have the possibility of preventing the foreclosure.

You can sell the property yourself or you can consider filing for bankruptcy to stop the foreclosure process. I talk more about bankruptcy in Chapter 6. You may also be able to refinance or work out a payment plan. I talk more about these options in Chapter 5.

Question 17: **How do most lenders handle delinquent loans?**

When your mortgage payment is between 35 and 45 days late, you will get a Borrower Information Packet from the bank that indicates the status of your mortgage. You will also get information about how you can "cure" the default; in other words, various options you have to get your payments back on track.

In the packet there should be a toll-free number for calling your lender. You should also get a brochure titled "How to Avoid Foreclosure," from HUD (U.S. Department of Housing and Urban Development). You can get a copy of this brochure online at *http://www.hud.gov/foreclosure/index.cfm.*

Don't ignore this package or any other letter from your lender. Call or write your lender's loss mitigation department as soon as possible. Be ready to explain your situation and provide any financial information they may request so they can help you. This can include your monthly income and expenses, your income (or lack of it), and other information related to your financial situation.

You should stay in your home during the entire length of the pre-foreclosure process. You may not qualify for assistance if you leave your property.

You can also contact a HUD-approved housing counseling agency at (800) 569-4287. These agencies have information on services and programs offered by government agencies, as well as by private and community organizations, that could help you save your home.

Question 18: **What are demand letters?**

If you get a letter that states the entire balance of your loan is due and payable immediately, that is called a "demand letter." It's sometimes called a "notice of acceleration," because it is based on the acceleration clause of your mortgage contract. This clause describes the situations under which you are considered in default or late on your payments. If the clause does exist in your mortgage, it allows the lender to accelerate, or push forward, the date that your mortgage must be paid in full.

If you don't pay the loan in full by the date specified in your demand letter, the lender does have the right to foreclose on your mortgage, but it must comply with the requirements specified in your loan documents as well as other relevant laws in your state. If you get a demand letter, your first call should be to seek advice from an attorney regarding your next steps.

Question 19: **What is default status?**

Once your mortgage payments are 90 days late, your loan will be considered in default status and the foreclosure process can begin. Before you get to that status, however, your loan will go into delinquent status. Your mortgage loan will be in delinquent status after you miss two scheduled monthly payments.

Most lenders will transfer the servicing of your loan from the regular servicer to a special servicer once you've missed two payments. You will get a letter in the mail, as indicated in the answer to Question 17, which will give you an 800 number for contacting this special servicer, who is often in the loss mitigation department.

The special servicer is the one who will decide what the best workout strategy is for your loan. How cooperative you are with this special servicer can determine whether or not the servicer will work with you to delay the decision to foreclose on this loan and give you the opportunity to consider other workout strategies. In Chapter 5, I talk about possible workout strategies to stop foreclosure.

Question 20: Can a loan be reinstated that is in default status?

In most states, you have from the time you receive notice that your mortgage is in default to five days prior to the foreclosure sale to reinstate your loan. The simplest way to reinstate your mortgage loan is to pay all past-due payments and other costs in full.

If you are able to borrow money from a relative or friend to reinstate your loan, you should call your special servicer or other lender contact and ask for a "reinstatement statement." This statement will list all past-due amounts and the total you must pay to reinstate your loan.

If you can't pay the amount due in full, you may be able to negotiate a payment arrangement for the past-due amounts and begin repaying your monthly payments. You may also be able to work out a Special Forbearance Agreement (read Question 38) or a repayment plan whereby a portion of the past-due amount is added to your regular monthly payment for a specified period of time until all past-due amounts are paid in full.

Question 21: **What is lis pendens?**

Lis pendens is Latin for "a suit pending." This term can refer to any pending lawsuit, but when it is filed concerning real estate, it indicates to any potential buyer or lender that there is a lawsuit pending involving the title to the property or a claim of ownership interest in the property.

This notice is filed with the county land records office. The time period from when a lawsuit is filed until the time the case is actually heard in court is called lis pendens. Once the county records a lis pendens against a piece of property, all are alerted that the property's title is in question. This does make the property less attractive to a buyer or lender.

If someone decides to buy the property after the lis pendens is filed, the person who takes ownership of the property will be subject to the ultimate decision of the lawsuit.

Question 22: **What is a Notice of Default?**

A Notice of Default, which for most conventional loans is sent when you are 90 to 95 days past your last loan payment, sets the process of foreclosure in motion. Once a lender notifies you that you are in default, it directs its attorney or trustee to initiate the foreclosure process. The Notice of Default is used during a non-judicial foreclosure action (see Question 32).

Normally you will be given three months before an actual sale takes place and up to five days before the sale to reinstate your account, but this depends on state law. I review the foreclosure process for each state in Chapter 10.

The letter of default will also state the amount due as of a specific date and that the amount will increase until your account becomes current. You are also instructed on how to get a statement of the full amount due at any time during the three-month period you are in default prior to the sale of the property. You will also find instructions telling you how to stop the sale of the property by paying the full amount due.

Question 23: **How does a Notice of Default work?**

After you have been sent a Notice of Default, the lender's attorney files the notice in the county in which the property is located. This becomes public record for all to see. It gives the public constructive notice that a mortgage or deed is in default and provides the schedule for a foreclosure sale. (In most cases, the sale occurs through a private trustee's auction.)

The Notice of Default is then sent by certified or registered mail, postage prepaid and return receipt requested, to the current owner, mortgagors of record, and all dwelling units that are secured by the mortgage in default. All other lien holders are sent information about the foreclosure sale as well.

Question 24: **How can I cure my home loan if it is in default?**

The simplest way to cure your home loan if it is in default is to pay the amount past due in full. You may be able to borrow funds from a friend or family member. You also may be able to work out payments with your lender. I discuss options for saving your home in Chapter 5.

Question 25: **What information is included in a foreclosure notice?**

A foreclosure notice contains detailed information about the borrower, the property, and the loan involved in the foreclosure. This information includes:

- Date that the Notice of Default or lawsuit (lis pendens) was filed and recorded in the public records
- Names and addresses of the mortgagor or trustor whose loan is in default
- Names and addresses of the lender, trustee, or beneficiary who are foreclosing on the loan

- Notice of Default or case number
- Street address of the property
- Legal description of the property
- The land use or zoning code for the property
- The value of the property in the tax assessor's records
- Original amount of the loan
- The date the original loan was made
- The date the last payment was made on the loan
- The amount of the payments that are past due
- The balance of the loan at the time the foreclosure action is filed
- The date of the public foreclosure auction or trustee's sale

Question 26: **Will notice of my pending foreclosure be published in the newspaper?**

The Notice of Default and information about the foreclosure sale is published once a week for at least three successive calendar weeks before the date of the foreclosure sale in most states. The publication chosen for this notice must have general circulation in the county or counties in which the property in question is located.

The newspaper chosen will be conducive to providing notice of foreclosure to interested parties. Your attorney will know which newspaper is likely to be used. If there is no newspaper appropriate for this circulation, a Notice of Default or foreclosure will be posted at the courthouse of the county or counties in which the property is located and at the place where the property sale will be held.

Question 27: **What is a loan reinstatement period?**

Your loan reinstatement period begins when your Notice of Default is filed with the county and ends five business days before the foreclosure sale in most states. During this period you can stop the foreclosure process by bringing your loan current.

You bring your loan current by paying all past-due payments, as well as any penalties. If you are able to find the money to do this, possibly by borrowing from family or friends, you should ask your trustee or lender for a reinstatement statement. This statement will detail all funds that are owed.

If you are able to get some of the money but can't pay the amount due in full, you may be able to negotiate a partial payment agreement with your lender. I talk about repayment options in Chapter 5.

Question 28: **What is a mortgage estoppel letter?**

A mortgage estoppel letter from the trustor or lender verifies the type of loan, any unpaid principal loan balance, interest rate, principal and interest payment, insurance payment, tax payment, payment due date, escrow impound balance, and total monthly payment. It will also include the amount of loan payments past due; the total amount of accrued interest; the late charges, penalties, and legal fees owed; and the total amount needed to cure the default and reinstate your mortgage loan.

This is a legal process that lays out all the terms so a party to the transaction can't later change the rules and ask for more money. If you are thinking about selling your home to avoid foreclosure, you likely will need to request an estoppel letter from your trustee or lender's loss mitigation department. This gives the buyer a guarantee that he or she is getting full information about your loan so there are no surprises at closing.

Question 29: **What must my lender do before foreclosing on or repossessing my home?**

The first step in the process toward a loan foreclosure is to send a Notice of Default (for a non-judicial foreclosure) or file a lawsuit (for a judicial foreclosure). I talk more about the process for both types of foreclosures in the following questions.

Once these acts are filed with the county in which the property is located, and if you are in a state that allows non-judicial foreclosure, then you enter into a reinstatement period, which is a period of about three months before your home is sold by the trustee or lender at auction.

If you don't pay all outstanding debt in full during the reinstatement period or work out some other payment arrangement with your trustee or lender, a Notice of Trustee Sale, which gives the date, time, and location of the sale of your property, will be recorded and sent to you. For full details of the non-judicial foreclosure process, see Question 33.

If you are in a state that requires a judicial foreclosure process, see Question 31 for more details about how that process works.

Question 30: **What is judicial foreclosure?**

Lenders must use the judicial foreclosure process if it is required in the state in which the property is located. Chapter 10 reviews the foreclosure rules of each state. A judicial foreclosure requires a court action to repossess a person's property. This type of foreclosure is required when a trust deed or mortgage does not have a "power of sale" clause, which means the lender must take the borrower to court. This can be a much more lengthy and costly process than is a non-judicial foreclosure.

The judicial foreclosure process starts when a lender files a lawsuit to foreclose and names the borrower in default, which could be a mortgagor or trustor, as the defendant. Other defendants could be any lien holders of record that have an interest in the property.

Question 31: **How does the judicial foreclosure process work?**

Once a lawsuit has been filed by the lender, the borrower and any other defendants usually have 20 days to reply formally to the lawsuit and present their case. If there is no reply to the suit, the judge rules against the defendant and orders that the mortgage or deed of trust be foreclosed on and the property sold at auction. So, if you get a notice that a lawsuit or lis pendens has been filed with the county, get thee to an attorney quickly.

Your attorney will reply to the lawsuit on your behalf and a court hearing date will be set. The timing of this hearing varies state by state and depending on the backlog of cases in your state. Once the case is heard in court, the judge will either order that the loan be foreclosed on or will dismiss the case.

If the judge rules against you and orders the loan to be foreclosed on, the public foreclosure auction sale will be scheduled by the county sheriff or other party designated for that purpose by the county in which the property is located.

Public foreclosure auction sales will be advertised and the property will be sold to the highest bidder at the auction or taken back by the lender if there are no acceptable bids from the auction participants. The judge may also award the lender a deficiency judgment against the borrower if the bid that is accepted is less than the amount owed.

After the sale you may be able to exercise statutory redemption rights if permitted in your state. To exercise these rights you must pay off the entire unpaid balance of your loan plus late fees, penalties, attorney fees, and trustee costs. While you don't have the legal right to reinstate your loan during the redemption period, some lenders may still permit you to do so.

If there is a statutory redemption period, the sheriff's deed or certificate of title is given to the highest bidder as soon as that period expires. If there is no statutory redemption period, then the highest bidder will get the deed or title immediately after the sale.

Question 32: **What is non-judicial foreclosure?**

A non-judicial foreclosure permits the lender or trustee to foreclose on your property without having to go to court by invoking the power of sale clause in your mortgage or deed of trust. If a non-judicial foreclosure is permitted, you will have a power of sale clause in your mortgage or trust documents.

Question 33: **How does the non-judicial foreclosure process work?**

A non-judicial foreclosure starts after the Notice of Default is sent to the borrower, who can be a mortgagor or trustor, and filed with the county or counties in which the property is located. After the Notice of Default is filed, the borrower then has about a three-month period to reinstate the loan. The actual time period involved for reinstatement and public trustee sale varies state by state, but I'm including the most common time periods here. See Chapter 10 for details about your state.

About 20 to 25 days before the end of the reinstatement period, a public trustee's sale date is set and a Notice of Trustee Sale is recorded with the county or counties in which the property is located. The Notice of Trustee Sale is also sent to the borrower. The public trustee's sale is then advertised.

The property will be sold to the highest bidder at the public trustee's sale or taken back by the lender if there are no acceptable bids from the public. If there are statutory redemption rights after the sale, the buyer will be given time to redeem his or her property based on these rights. To redeem the property the buyer must pay off the entire balance of the loan, plus all late fees, penalties, attorney fees, and trustee's costs. Although your reinstatement rights ended before the trustee sale, some lenders may allow you to reinstate the loan during the redemption period.

Question 34: What is power of sale foreclosure?

A power of sale foreclosure is one in which a power of sale clause exists in the mortgage or deed of trust. This clause will specify exactly what steps are needed in order to foreclose on the property.

When a power of sale clause does exist, the procedures for a non-judicial foreclosure, as discussed in Question 33, are followed. For a non-judicial foreclosure to go forward, the loan default must be proven and the borrower must be notified using a Notice of Default.

Question 35: What is a "no power of sale" foreclosure?

If there is no power of sale clause in the mortgage or deed of trust, then a no power of sale foreclosure must be started. If the property is in a state where judicial foreclosures are required, then the process of a no power of sale foreclosure must follow the steps discussed in Question 31.

Question 36: How do FHA and DVA foreclosure rules differ from conventional loans?

Both FHA (Federal Housing Administration) and DVA (Department of Veterans Affairs) home mortgages are backed by the United States government, which means the government will reimburse the bank for 100 percent of the loan if a borrower defaults on the mortgage.

In the case of FHA loans, these reimbursements come out of an account that is funded by insurance premiums collected at mortgage closings. Borrowers must pay the insurance premium at closing (which is usually financed as part of the mortgage). The insurance premiums are then paid into a fund that is used to pay off lenders if a borrower defaults. In the case of DVA loans, the loan guarantee is a benefit offered all veterans, for which they do not need to pay any premiums. The government pays any loan defaults.

For both types of loans, you will have access to extensive counseling to try to keep you in your home and avoid foreclosure.

Question 37: How does the FHA counsel borrowers on the verge of defaulting?

You don't have to wait until you are facing foreclosure to seek help from a HUD (U.S. Department of Housing and Urban Development) housing counseling agency. Agencies are located in every state and can provide you with assistance on defaults and credit issues, as well as foreclosures.

You can get help on alternatives such as home equity conversion mortgage counseling, loss mitigation, relocation counseling, money and debt management, mortgage delinquency, and default resolution counseling. You can also get advice on how to avoid a predatory lender. Some counseling agencies are also charity organizations and may be able to help you with financial assistance to get through a bad period.

To find a HUD counseling agency near you go to *www.hud. gov/offices/hsg/sfh/hcc/hcs.cfm* or look in your local phone book for the number of the HUD office nearest you.

Question 38: What is special forbearance?

If you've lost your job or are experiencing another type of temporary loss of income or unexpected financial expense, such as a health emergency, you may be able to request a Special Forbearance Agreement from your lender if you have an FHA loan. The agreement may reduce or delay your monthly payments for a specified period of time. This process is called a special forbearance. In order for a special forbearance to be requested you must have at least three payments due and unpaid.

In most cases this agreement will require that you repay any missed payments over a set number of months. These repayments will be added to your regular monthly payments as part of a repayment plan.

A special forbearance fails if the mortgagor abandons the property, the mortgagor advises the mortgagee that he or she will not follow through to fulfill the terms of agreement, or the mortgagor allows an installment that is part of the agreement to become due and unpaid for 60 consecutive days from the payment date. After that 60-day period, the mortgagee has 90 days to initiate a foreclosure.

If another financial crisis occurs during the period of time the agreement is in place, you can call and ask for an extension, and you also can ask for a renegotiation of the agreement. If you have become disabled and are waiting for your first monthly disability payment, you may be able to establish a Special Forbearance Agreement based on the start date of your disability payments.

Question 39: **What is a mortgage modification?**

Mortgage modification is an alternative to foreclosure if you are a mortgagor with an FHA loan and have experienced a financial hardship. The modification can be used if you have accessible income after the hardship, but won't have sufficient income to continue to pay the original loan as agreed.

Your mortgage payments must be 90 days or more past due for a lender to consider a mortgage modification. When a mortgage goes into default, HUD expects mortgagees to offer formal or informal forbearance relief.

Once the mortgagor recovers from the financial hardship, the lender must then determine if the mortgagor can resume the original mortgage payments and repay the amount past due in a reasonable amount of time. If the mortgagor cannot afford to pay the original mortgage payments, the lender must determine whether the mortgagor is eligible for a mortgage modification or a streamline refinanced mortgage, which means you won't need as much documentation to qualify for the loan.

Question 40: What is a partial claim on an FHA mortgage?

A partial claim is an option that you may be able to use to reinstate a delinquent FHA mortgage. If you qualify, your lender will advance funds in an amount necessary to reinstate the loan, but it cannot exceed the equivalent of 12 months of total payments including principal, interest, taxes, and insurance (PITI). To qualify you must prove that you can make the payments and that you will continue occupying the property as a primary residence.

The partial claim will be executed using a promissory note payable to HUD that will be subordinate to the mortgage. You cannot be charged any additional fees for this option. However, if you were facing a foreclosure action and that action was canceled because you chose to use the partial claim option, you will be charged legal costs and fees related to the canceled foreclosure action.

Partial claim notes do not accrue interest and are not due and payable until the mortgagor either pays off the first mortgage or no longer owns the property. If you do decide to sell the property, you must include the amount of the partial claim when calculating the total indebtedness on the property.

Question 41: What is a HUD-approved housing counselor?

A HUD-approved housing counselor provides information about HUD-approved options for a homeowner seeking assistance. The counselor follows a seven-step process:

- Conducts an interview with the homeowner to collect basic information about the homeowner and his or her needs or problems.
- Identifies any resources within the counseling agency, HUD, or in the homeowner's community that might be able to help the homeowner resolve the problem.
- Designs a counseling plan for the homeowner.
- Discusses the plan with the homeowner and obtains the homeowner's permission to carry out the plan. This will include actions the homeowner must take.
- Refers the homeowner to resources that are available to him or her within the community. The counselor will also assist with making appointments with the agencies that might be able to help.
- Finds and recommends any additional private or group counseling sessions conducted by the counseling agency or other community.
- Monitors the homeowner's progress toward resolving the problems.

You can find a HUD-approved housing counseling agency by calling (800) 569-4287 or using the online search tool (*www.hud .gov/offices/hsg/sfh/hcc/hcs.cfm*) to find a counselor near your home.

Question 42: **How does the VA counsel borrowers on the verge of defaulting?**

If you have a VA loan and are in serious financial trouble, your first call should be to find the VA Regional Loan Center near you. You can find one by calling (800) 827-1000. These centers employ people who are familiar with the VA loan process and can provide financial counseling to help you avoid foreclosure.

Do not seek help from a stranger who agrees to make your back payments provided that you sign a piece of paper. Before signing anything, be sure to contact your lender or the Loan Guaranty Division of the nearest VA regional office.

Often these offers of help from strangers are scams in which you sign a deed and can't get the property back unless you agree to buy it back at a much higher price. If you don't agree to the terms of the contract, the person can take possession of your home.

Question 43: What is the borrower's right to reinstate after acceleration?

If you have received a notice that your loan is due in full, that is an acceleration notice, which may be allowed by the acceleration clause in your loan agreement. Even after you receive this notice you do have the right to reinstate your loan, which can be done any time before whichever date is earliest:

- Five days before the sale of the property under a power of sale included in the loan agreement.
- The day required by applicable law in your state for the termination of your right to reinstate.
- A court judgment that enforces your loan agreement.

You can have your loan agreement reinstated by paying everything you owe under your loan agreement as if no acceleration had happened. You will also need to pay any legal fees or court costs incurred after your loan was in default. In addition, you will need to assure that you will be able to make all future payments.

Your lender can require that you pay for the reinstatement in cash, by money order, by certified check, by bank check, by treasurer's check, or by cashier's check. You may also be allowed to pay by electronic funds transfer.

Once you pay all money due, the loan agreement will remain in effect as if no acceleration had happened. But, you cannot sell or transfer any interest in your property without the permission of your lender as part of an agreement to get the cash you need.

Question 44: What is a "due on sale" or acceleration clause?

The due on sale or acceleration clause is a provision in your loan agreement or promissory note specifying that when a certain event happens, such as not making your payments on time, the lender has the right to require that the entire amount due be paid immediately. This is a common clause in documents used for the purchase of real property.

The due on sale or acceleration clause can require that the property be sold in order to pay the note immediately. Some states prohibit the due on sale clause and instead allow a new property owner to assume the debt. You can find out more about your state's rules in Chapter 10.

Question 45: What are the acceleration remedies?

If a lender intends to impose the due on sale or acceleration clause, there are a number of remedies that must be offered to the borrower first. These include sending a notice prior to acceleration indicating that there is a breach of the loan agreement and how the borrower can cure the breach.

The borrower must be given a date that is not less than 10 days from the date of the notice by which the breach can be cured. The notice will also state that if the borrower fails to cure the breach on or before the date specified, this may result in the acceleration of all sums due and require the sale of the property.

The notice must also inform the borrower that he or she has the right to reinstate the loan agreement after acceleration. The borrower must also be told of his or her right to bring a court action if the borrower believes the default is an error or for any other defense the borrower might have in regard to the acceleration and sale of his or her property.

Question 46: **What is a foreclosure moratorium?**

A foreclosure moratorium is one type of assistance that can be offered homeowners in the area affected by a natural disaster as declared by the president. When a foreclosure moratorium is designated by FEMA, all FHA-approved lenders are prohibited from initiating new foreclosures. Lenders are encouraged to take actions that assist borrowers with hazard and flood insurance filings, waiver of late charges, and mortgage modification agreements.

In most cases when a foreclosure moratorium is declared, two other federal agencies, Freddie Mac and Fannie Mae, will also impose a foreclosure moratorium for borrowers who own homes in the disaster area. Freddie Mac and Fannie Mae provide a large share of the money for private mortgages not under the FHA or VA loan programs.

Question 47: **What is a deficiency judgment?**

After a property is sold at auction following a foreclosure, sometimes the amount due does not cover the full amount due the lender. Any difference between the amount netted at a sale and the amount owed to the lender is called a deficiency. The lender can go to court and ask for a deficiency judgment in some states.

The deficiency judgment is the result of a lawsuit that was filed by the lender. If you receive papers indicating that a lawsuit has been filed, you should contact an attorney immediately. You will have to respond to the lawsuit within 30 days. If you don't answer the suit, the judge can assume that you have no defense, and you will lose your case by default. Even if you believe you don't really owe the money, the judge can issue a deficiency judgment if you don't respond to the filing of the suit. A deficiency judgment will affect your credit report.

Question 48: **Can I be evicted from my home?**

Yes, you can be evicted from your home, but only through the standard eviction process in your state. You should stay in your home from the time you first receive notice of a deficiency until the time you are ordered out. If you abandon the home it's much easier for the foreclosure process to proceed. In order to reinstate a loan, the home must be your primary residence.

You can stay in your home even after the ownership has been transferred to the highest bidder. After a foreclosure you automatically become a tenant in the house you previously owned. You can rent the home from the new owner or the owner can start legal procedures for your eviction.

You likely will lose your home after a foreclosure. You should check on the eviction rules for your state so you know what to expect. In many states the new owner can send you a legal notice asking you to leave the premises within 72 hours. If you don't leave the home within 72 hours, the new owner must file a case in court and ask the judge to evict you. The judge will decide whether or not you are to be evicted and how long you may stay in the home. If you are willing and able to pay rent, a judge will usually give you more time. If you don't like the judge's decision, you have 10 days to appeal it.

Question 49: **How long does an eviction take?**

From the day you get the eviction notice, the amount of time before a court official (usually the county sheriff) comes to pack you up and move you and your possessions out of the house can take as little as six weeks to as long as six months, depending on where you live. The average amount of time is usually about 10 weeks.

Chapter 3

LOOKING AT LIENS

There are many different types of liens that can be placed against your property. Not all of them result in a foreclosure. In this chapter, I review the different types of liens and how they may impact your risk of facing foreclosure. Even if foreclosure isn't a possibility, a lien can make it difficult for you to sell your property, refinance it, or transfer it to another owner.

Question 50: What are statutory liens?

Statutory liens are those that creditors can use to obtain a security interest in your assets to satisfy a debt based on state and sometimes federal laws. The two most commonly used statutory liens are mechanic's liens (which can be filed by someone who worked on your home) and tax liens. If you try to sell property on which a statutory lien has been placed, the debtor will have to be paid from the sales proceeds to remove the lien.

A statutory lien will be considered invalid if it has not been filed with the appropriate government office, a process also known as "perfected." Mechanic's liens usually must be filed within 60 to 90 days after the work is performed and acted on within one year. See Question 57 for more detail about the process for mechanic's liens. Tax liens can be filed up to two to three years after the taxes are due. If a tax lien is not paid, the government can foreclose on the property and sell it for the value of the taxes.

Question 51: What are equitable liens?

If you have an equitable lien against your property, it means there is a lien against the property, but it will stay in your possession. The lien holder cannot foreclose on the property.

An equitable lien can be express or implied. An express equitable lien is one based on a written contract. An implied equitable lien is one that must be declared by a court and is based on the conduct and dealings of the parties. Whether an express or implied equitable lien, the property in question remains in the possession of the debtor, but the property owner cannot remove or change the property without the permission of the lien holder.

Question 52: What are specific liens?

A specific lien is any lien that is placed against a certain property. There are many different types of specific liens, including a mechanic's lien, trust deed, attachment, property tax lien, and lis pendens. These differ from a general lien, which affects all property of an owner, such as a judgment lien or federal or state income tax liens.

Question 53: What are general liens?

A general lien comes from everyday transactions that you engage in as part of your general course of business rather than relating to a specific transaction or property. In business, those types of professionals who do work for you, such as attorneys, accountants, or bankers, are most likely to use a general lien.

For example, when an attorney or accountant wants to be certain to be paid for his or her work, the professional can retain possession of papers and personal property that you have given him or her in order to perform those professional services until payment is received. This would be considered a general lien.

Question 54: **What are real property tax liens?**

You can end up with a real property tax lien placed against your property by the city or county government if you fail to pay your property taxes. The amount of the lien will be based on the past-due taxes, as well as any interest and penalties.

If you don't pay the lien in two to three years after your taxes are past due, the tax collector of the city or county can foreclose on the tax lien and sell the property at a tax deed sale. At least 30 days prior to the sale date, the county clerk will advertise a tax deed sale listing the properties that will be available for sale. Most counties hold tax deed sales about once or twice a month.

Question 55: **What are federal tax liens?**

If you owe back taxes to the federal government and don't pay them after the IRS has demanded payment, the IRS can attach a federal tax lien to the property. In order to do this, the IRS must file a Notice of Federal Tax Lien at the county or state office where the property subject to the lien is located. The filing of a federal tax lien is the core of the type of collection action the IRS can take to recover back taxes.

The IRS is not required to notify or make a public announcement regarding the existence of a federal tax lien, so this lien is sometimes known as the "secret lien." It exists as a matter of law and can be perfected even without filing a notice. Tax liens usually have to be filed within two to three years of the tax delinquency, and expire after ten. But that doesn't mean you're off the hook. The IRS can refile the lien within one year after the lien expires.

The federal government can foreclose on the lien and force the sale of the property. A federal tax lien supersedes state law, so any homestead or other protection provided in your state will not stand against a federal action. If the federal government does decide to foreclose on your property, you will receive a Notice of Seizure, Foreclosure or Auction.

Question 56: How can I have a federal tax lien removed from the property's title?

In order to get a federal tax lien removed from your property, you must first either pay your back taxes plus any penalties or interest in full or work out a compromise agreement that includes the removal of your federal tax lien. You may also be able to sign a bond with the IRS guaranteeing payment. If the IRS accepts that bond, you can get the federal tax lien removed. If your property is involved, your best bet is to work with an attorney on the removal of the tax lien.

Within 30 days after you pay off the IRS or have it adjusted, the IRS will submit a notice to the county to remove the tax lien. The IRS should file a Certificate of Release of Federal Tax Lien with your county. If that is not done, you can call (800) 913-6050 for assistance. You may have to pay fees related to the release of the lien charged by your state or county.

Question 57: What are mechanic's liens?

Any time you have work done on your home by a contractor, architect, surveyor, or mechanic and you don't pay for the work, a mechanic's lien can be filed against your property with the county clerk in the county where the property is located.

This type of lien is a secured interest in your property. If you don't pay off the debt, the lien holder can foreclose on the property and force the sale of the property.

Sometimes when you hire a contractor, he or she in turn hires subcontractors to do the work. The contractor also buys materials from suppliers for the work on your property. You pay the contractor, but he or she does not pay the subcontractors or suppliers. Any of the subcontractors or suppliers who weren't paid can place a mechanic's lien on your home. Be sure you know who did work on the home and ask for a lien release from all potential lien claimants before you pay the contractor. You can find a good example of a lien release on the California Contractors State License Board Web site (*www.cslb.ca.gov/forms/LienRelease Forms.pdf*).

A mechanic's lien will be invalid unless it has been filed with the appropriate government office (perfected) and foreclosed on in the appropriate time. Typically, a lien must be filed within 60 or 90 days of when the work was done. The contractor then has one year to ask for a foreclosure and force the sale of the home to collect his or her debt. If a mechanic's lien is placed on your home, contact an attorney to assess your options. In some cases the lien may not be valid.

Question 58: What are judgment liens?

A judicial lien can be granted by the court to your creditor, which gives your creditor an interest in your property in order to satisfy a debt, such as the repayment of an award for damages. This debt can be based on your credit spending, but there are also numerous other reasons a judgment lien can be placed against your property.

For example, suppose you were driving a car and caused an accident for which the police determined you were at fault, and you caused injury to someone. The injured person could sue you, and if he wins the suit, a judgment lien could be placed against your property.

The lien holder could foreclose on your property and force a sale in order to collect his money if you don't pay voluntarily.

If a judgment lien is placed against your home, contact an attorney immediately to assess the situation and determine your options for protecting your home. Most judgment liens must be foreclosed on within 10 to 20 years or they expire.

Question 59: **How can I contest the validity of a judgment lien?**

You will need an attorney to contest the validity of the judgment lien. If you want to contest the court ruling upon which the judgment lien is based, your attorney would need to appeal the ruling, usually in 60 to 90 days after the ruling has taken place, so act quickly if you do want to appeal the judge's decision.

For example, you may dispute the amount of the debt involved and you would need to prove on appeal that the judgment was not based on accurate information. In many states you would have homestead protections in place that can prevent a lien holder from taking your home. You likely would have to file bankruptcy to stop a foreclosure based on a judgment lien.

Question 60: **What is a consensual lien?**

Any lien to which you voluntarily consent is called a consensual lien. The most common type of consensual lien is a mortgage. For example, as a home buyer you consent to give the bank a security interest in your home in exchange for the money you need to buy the home. This type of consensual lien is called a purchase-money security interest lien.

Another type of lien is called the non-purchase-money security interest lien. When you consent to this type of lien, it usually involves property you own that you use as collateral in exchange for a loan. Examples of this type of lien are a second mortgage or an equity line of credit.

Both of these types of liens are usually considered non-possessory, which means that as the debtor you still own the property and it is titled in your name. But some consensual liens can be possessory. For example, if you pawn a watch in exchange for a loan from a pawnbroker, he or she will likely take possession of the watch until you repay the loan.

Question 61: What are mortgage and "deed of trust" liens?

You agree to a mortgage or deed of trust lien voluntarily when you buy a house, or other property, and pledge the property as security for the repayment of the debt. If you don't make the payments, the lender can foreclose on your security instrument, which is the mortgage or deed of trust lien.

Once the lender takes all the necessary steps to foreclose on the property, whether by judicial or non-judicial means (read Chapter 2 for more information about these means), he or she can force the sale of your home at a public foreclosure auction or trustee's sale. The foreclosure process does vary by state. In Chapter 10, I review the rules for each of the states.

Question 62: What are state inheritance tax liens?

Many states levy an inheritance tax against the estate of a deceased person. If the money is not paid, the amount of the inheritance tax becomes a lien against the estate.

Some states do allow inheritance tax exemptions, so tax rates can differ depending upon who received the property. For example, a deceased spouse will likely be taxed at a lower rate than will a friend of the deceased. Some states are starting to phase out state inheritance taxes.

If a state inheritance tax lien is placed against a piece of property you own, or even plan to buy, the sale of the property can be forced by court order to pay the inheritance taxes.

Question 63: **What are corporate franchise tax liens?**

Some states collect corporate franchise tax. This tax is imposed on corporations who want the right to conduct business within the state. If a corporation fails to pay its franchise tax, the state can file a lien against any real property in the state that belongs to the corporation.

Question 64: **What are bail bond liens?**

If you or a family member needs to be bailed out of jail and you put up your house for collateral, the bail company is likely to place a bail bond lien against your property. This lien is a type of insurance policy for the court. If the person who was bailed out doesn't show up in court, the amount of the bond is paid to the court by the bail bond company and a warrant is issued for the arrest of the person who didn't appear.

A bail bond lien is usually secured using a deed of trust, which enables the bail bond company to foreclose on your property if you don't repay the expenses of the bail bond company. The deed of trust will be recorded in the county where the property is located.

The bail bond company can also foreclose on the property if you do not pay the bond premium to which you agreed. Because the bond is similar to insurance, you will have bond premiums to pay plus any accrued interest. Most bail bond premiums are for a period of one year. If the trial for the case in question takes longer, then you would need to renew the premium for each year involved.

Be sure that during the final court appearance, at the end of the case, the defendant's attorney asks the court to release (exonerate) the bond. The bonding company won't remove the lien until the bond is exonerated. In addition, to get the lien removed you must have paid all premiums and any interest due. Once the court has ordered the bond exonerated and you have paid all premiums, the bail bond company has 30 days to send you a "reconveyance," which is a document that officially releases the lien against your property. Once you get that reconveyance, be sure you have it recorded with the county as well, in order to clear your property title.

Question 65: **What are code enforcement liens?**

If you get a notice from a local or county government agency indicating that your property does not meet code, the government entity can fine you for not complying. If you fail to pay the fine, a code enforcement lien can be placed against your property.

There are several types of code enforcement liens that can be placed against your property, depending on the type of violation and the level of abatement required. The common types include:

- **Notice of Abatement Proceedings:** This type of lien does not specify the dollar amount required to remove the lien. This notice notifies prospective buyers or lenders that violations exist on the property.
- **Partial Abatement Lien:** After administrative abatement hearings, a hearing officer will order the property owner to correct a violation and assess payment to cover costs and penalties for failure to correct the code violation. This lien notifies the public of the violation and can prevent the sale or refinancing of the property. It sometimes can stop the owner from getting insurance on the property as well.
- **Supplemental Abatement Lien:** This lien is recorded when additional costs are incurred after the partial lien is recorded.
- **Notice of Lis Pendens:** This lien notifies the public that a lawsuit has been filed and is in addition to a partial abatement lien or notice of abatement proceedings.

Question 66: What is a fraudulent lien?

If someone files a lien against your property based on information that is not true, it is a fraudulent lien. A fraudulent lien is not enforceable. In fact, a lien holder who willfully exaggerated the amount claimed in a lien can be held responsible to the owner for all damages incurred because of the filing of the lien plus punitive damages. The filing of a fraudulent lien is a criminal offense that constitutes a felony in most states.

Question 67: What is slander of title?

If someone publishes false and malicious statements regarding your title to real estate, this could be considered a slander of title. To prove your case you will need to prove that the statement is false and that the statement was made with malicious intent. To collect damages, you will need to prove that the statement caused actual or special damages, which are damages that are a natural consequence of the slander, such as the salability or loss of use of the property.

Question 68: What are municipal liens?

If you fail to pay for municipal services, such as water, sewage, or trash removal, your local government entity can place a municipal lien against your property for the money owed. Any lien imposed by the authority of a municipal government is a municipal lien.

Municipal liens are also used for major improvements done by the city or county. For example, suppose the city decides to put in new sidewalks. Each property in the area where the sidewalks are to be built may have a municipal lien placed against the property for its share of the costs. The lien is lifted when the county assessment is paid off in full by the homeowner.

Question 69: **What are welfare liens?**

If you collect welfare payments from state or federal government agencies and it is later determined that you were not legally entitled to those welfare payments, the government agency can file a welfare lien against your home.

The government entity can approve the sale of your home for the amount of the welfare lien. Whoever buys the home would have to satisfy any other liens, including your mortgage.

Question 70: **What are public defender liens?**

If you needed the services of a court-ordered public defender and were not able to pay for those services, a public defender lien can be placed against your property by the local, state, or federal government. The amount of the lien will be set by the judge of the circuit court or the magistrate judge at a reasonable amount for the services rendered.

Question 71: **What are marital support liens?**

If the court orders marital support payments and you don't make those payments, a lien can be placed against your property's title by the state and federal government. Foreclosure is not likely for the collection of a marital support lien, but if you have this type of lien placed against your property, you will have trouble selling or transferring the property.

Question 72: **What are child support liens?**

If you owe child support and don't pay it in full, the state or federal government can place a child support lien on your property until the past-due child support payments are made. In many states these liens can be placed without an additional court hearing.

While foreclosure is not likely to satisfy a lien, the child support lien must be paid in full when the property is sold or transferred. Failure to pay a child support lien can stall the sale or transfer of property.

Question 73: **What are homeowners' association liens?**

If you own a piece of property that is located inside the boundaries of a homeowners' association, you will be required to pay fees to the association. These fees are usually determined at annual meetings and assessed to each of the property owners to pay for upkeep, landscaping, roads, and other facilities offered by the association.

An association can place a homeowners' association lien against your property for any unpaid assessments. If you fail to pay, the association can foreclose on the property to collect the past-due payments.

Question 74: **What are subordinate lien holders?**

Subordinate lien holders include any person who holds a lien after the senior or first lien holder. In most cases the senior lien holder is the lender who financed the initial purchase of the property and holds the first mortgage.

Subordinate lien holders would include a lender who offered you a second mortgage or equity line loan. Other subordinate lien holders would include holders of liens mentioned previously.

The holder of the senior lien or first mortgage must be paid before subordinate lien holders can get their money. That is why in most cases, the interest rate is higher for a second mortgage or equity loan than it is for the first mortgage. The risk these lenders take is higher because they will only be paid after the first mortgage holder has been paid in full.

Chapter 4

REPORTING YOUR DELINQUENT LOAN

When you miss a payment, the information will be reported to a credit bureau or to the U.S. Department of Housing and Urban Development (HUD) or to both, depending upon the type of loan you have. All Federal Housing Administration (FHA) loans are reported delinquent within 30 days to HUD. Delinquencies on all types of mortgages are reported to the credit bureaus.

In this chapter, I review how the reporting systems work and what you can expect to find on your credit report about a delinquent loan.

Question 75: When must a lender report an FHA delinquency to HUD?

Your lender must report your FHA loan delinquent to HUD once your loan is 30 days late. All reporting is done on the fifth business day of the next month using a system called the Single Family Default Monitoring System (SFDMS).

This information provides HUD with the up-to-date status of all HUD-insured mortgages. HUD uses the information to monitor trends in the mortgage market and keep an eye on default and foreclosure rates.

Every month, lenders must report any new delinquent cases and update the status of all previously reported cases. Monthly reporting continues on each delinquent loan until the lender reports that the loan is paid in full or the property is conveyed to HUD.

Question 76: **What is the Single Family Default Monitoring System?**

The Single Family Default Monitoring System (SFDMS) is a computer-based system that is used by all lenders who provide FHA loans to report any delinquent loans to HUD. Each loan is given a code depending on its status. These are some common codes for delinquent loans:

- **Status Code 42:** This is the code used the first time a loan is reported delinquent to HUD. The information indicating the first date a loan payment was missed sets the clock for all future action by the FHA to either get the borrower back on track through a repayment plan or other assistance or to foreclose on the property.
- **Status Code 67:** Mortgagor files for bankruptcy.
- **Status Code 69:** The bankruptcy court confirms the bankruptcy plan, if applicable.
- **Status Code 12:** Mortgagor is offered a Special Forbearance Agreement (see Question 38 for an explanation about Forbearance Agreements).
- **Status Code 76:** Bankruptcy is no longer a barrier to foreclosure.
- **Status Code 68:** Public legal action is initiated to foreclose on the property.

Question 77: **How does the lender report the status of my mortgage or other FHA home loan to the government?**

Within 30 days after your loan is delinquent, it will be reported to HUD. Your Social Security number is included as part of the reporting process. The information about your delinquent payments is then added to HUD's Credit Alert Interactive Voice Response System.

This system is used to determine your eligibility for any future HUD-insured mortgages. Delinquent loan case information remains in the HUD database for 12 months after the case is closed either by payoff or foreclosure.

When a lender accesses the database, it will be able to find out about any delinquent loans you may have and what the status of the loans currently are. If you've had a delinquency in the past that has been inactive (account closed, mortgage paid off, or home foreclosed), the lender will not be able to access the information using this database. The lender will have to access the information by ordering it through HUD archives.

Question 78: **How does a lender report the status of my mortgage or other home loan to the credit bureaus?**

Lenders are governed by numerous laws regarding what information can be reported to credit agencies. The two key acts that protect you as a consumer are the Privacy Act of 1974 (respect for your privacy) and the Debt Collection Act of 1982 as amended by the Debt Collection Improvement Act of 1996 (DCIA). The DCIA requires the reporting of all non-tax-delinquent consumer debt to credit reporting agencies. It also authorizes the reporting of current consumer and commercial debts.

If a lender intends to report you to the credit bureaus, he or she must first send notice within 60 days in advance of reporting you. I've found many lenders today put a statement regarding the reporting of delinquencies in the privacy information you receive when you first open your credit account or in the mortgage documents you receive when you close on your new home.

Reporting is usually done on a monthly basis by the middle of the next month after the delinquency. If your debt is to a government agency, the agency must first send you a notice indicating the intention to report the debt to the credit bureaus in 60 days. During that 60-day period you can either pay the debt in full or challenge the accuracy of the debt. If you ignore the notice, the debt will be reported to the credit bureaus.

Question 79: **How long does the delinquency show on my credit report?**

If you ask for a copy of your credit report for one of the credit reporting agencies, you will find monthly reporting on all your loans, including your mortgage. This report indicates whether you pay on time, if you have late payments (and how often you pay late), and if you are delinquent on any payments. You are also likely to find indication of any lawsuit settlements, judgments, or tax liens.

A delinquency, late payment, charge-off, or other negative entries, other than a bankruptcy, must be removed from your credit report once they are more than seven years old. A bankruptcy will show on a credit report for ten years, but any debts that are shown as past due that were wiped out by the bankruptcy must be removed after seven years.

You should challenge any information on your credit report that is not accurate or that is older than allowed by credit laws. If a credit agency continues after seven years to report debt that was charged off in a bankruptcy, you can ask for that reporting information to be removed.

Question 80: **How does a foreclosure impact my ability to buy another home in the future?**

As long as you can prove that you have the money to make payments, you likely will be able to buy another home in the future. But, while your foreclosure remains on your credit report, you will have to find a lender willing to take the risk.

It is likely that after a foreclosure, you will have to put more money down on your next home and will be required to pay a higher interest rate. For example, if home mortgage rates are 6.5 percent for a person who has a good credit history, you might have to pay 8.5 percent to get a loan if you lost a house to foreclosure in the past.

If your fortunes have improved and you've gotten past whatever financial crisis caused you to lose your home to foreclosure, don't hesitate to contact lenders to talk with them about your options. You should do some careful shopping to find the best deal and to ensure that you don't get caught up in a loan scam in which you risk facing foreclosure again.

Your best bet would be to work with a credit counselor who can assist you with establishing your credit. In Question 41 I talk about approved HUD housing counseling agencies. They can help with the process of buying a home, too.

Chapter 5

STOPPING FORECLOSURE ACTION

Foreclosure is not a foregone conclusion. Even if you have been warned that a lender is planning to start foreclosure proceedings, you still may be able to work out an alternative solution. Lenders really don't want to take possession of your home, so as long as you offer a reasonable alternative they will try to work something out with you. In this chapter I look at ways to stop foreclosure action.

Question 81: What is a foreclosure workout?

A foreclosure workout is essentially any solution you can work out with your lender to avoid a foreclosure. The most common solutions include a refinance, Special Forbearance Agreement (see Question 38), a mortgage modification (see Question 39), selling the home to someone else, a deed-in-lieu of foreclosure (see Question 90), and, as a last resort, bankruptcy.

Question 82: **Should I consider a debt consolidation loan?**

If you can stop a foreclosure by consolidating your debt, reducing your monthly payments to other creditors, and then having enough money to pay your mortgage lender, you should definitely consider that route. Not only will you improve your credit by getting all past-due loans up-to-date; you can save your home. The key problem is finding a lender who will do that for you. Be sure to avoid a predatory lender, which I talk about in the answer to the next question. But think twice about consolidating your debt, because you are converting unsecured debt (credit cards) to secured debt (an equity line) and putting your home ownership at risk of foreclosure.

Your best bet is to find a credit counselor who can assist you with sorting out your credit problems. You can find a good credit counselor near you at the Web site for the National Foundation for Credit Counseling (*www.debtadvice.org*) or you can call the foundation at (800) 388-2227.

Question 83: **What is a predatory lender?**

Predatory lenders charge high interest rates to borrowers and knowingly encourage borrowers to lie about their income, expenses, and cash available for down payments so they can qualify for a loan. In most cases they also charge fees for unnecessary products and services.

You could end up with a loan that has a balloon payment (for example, the full amount due in five years), an interest-only-payment loan (so you end up paying none of the principal due and sometimes not even all of the interest due, so your loan amount continues to increase), and steep pre-payment penalties (to make it expensive to pay off the loan when you find out how bad the deal is).

It's likely that you're dealing with a predatory lender if you are encouraged to lie on your application, or if you are asked to sign blank contracts or loan documents, or documents that include information that is not true. Another key sign is that you find the costs for the loan or other loan terms at closing are different from the terms you agreed to prior to closing.

Question 84: **What is a 125 percent LTV loan?**

A loan that is 125 percent LTV means that you are borrowing more than the appraised value of your home—25 percent more. That means that if you are unable to make the payments, you won't be able to sell your home for enough money to pay off the loan. You'll have to come up with additional cash at closing to pay off the loan in order to sell your home.

Equity line loans are frequently advertised for 125 percent LTV. Be careful before you consider one of those loans. Often, they are being offered by predatory lenders.

You also may not be able to write off all the interest you pay on these loans, as you are allowed to do with other mortgage debt. If you do have a 125 percent LTV equity loan, be sure to alert your tax adviser, so he or she can write off the interest appropriately. The last thing you need is the IRS questioning your deductions. That can be even more costly than the amount of tax you save by writing off the interest, if you have to go through an IRS audit just because you wrote off too much interest.

Question 85: **Can I ask for help from family or friends?**

While you can't borrow money from family and friends to help with a down payment when you first buy a home, there are no similar limits on asking for help if you need it to get caught up on a loan that is delinquent. Often this should be your first line of defense if you are trying to get yourself back on your feet after a financial disaster.

Question 86: **What is a short pay or short refinance?**

You may be able to work out a short pay or short refinance, which means that you, or someone representing you, negotiates with your lender to settle the loan for less than is due rather than foreclosing on the property. For example, suppose you owe $150,000 on the mortgage plus another $20,000 in past-due payments, interest, and legal fees.

You may be able to negotiate a settlement of the loan at $120,000 and then arrange for a refinance at $125,000 to cover the cost of paying off the original lender and also cover closing costs for the new loan.

A short pay or short refinance not only helps you avoid foreclosure; it also eliminates a portion of your debt. If you can't get your lender to agree to the full reduction in debt, you may be able to borrow enough money from family or friends to help make up the difference in paying off the original lender. Do be careful, though, to avoid a predatory lender for the loan refinance.

Question 87: **How can I modify my existing mortgage?**

You may be able to modify the original terms of your loan by working out a deal with your lender. This can include reducing your interest rate, reducing the amount of loan principal you pay with each payment, or extending the life of loan to reduce monthly payments. Many times these modifications are temporary solutions to help you recover from a financial emergency, such as the loss of a job or a severe medical emergency.

You may need to hire an attorney or a person who is a professional foreclosure negotiator to work out a modification with your lender. If you can't work out a modification on your own, don't hesitate to seek legal advice to save your home.

Question 88: **How can I set up a repayment plan?**

A repayment plan is a common way for you to work with your lender to avoid foreclosure, especially if the reason for your late payments was a temporary setback, such as a job or medical emergency. In most cases you will need to prove to your lender that you can now afford to make the payments in order to work out a payment plan.

Usually the lender will ask for income documentation. You will then need to pay some portion of the past-due payments, interest charges, and any costs or legal fees that may have been added on during the period of time you did not pay your loan.

You can then work out a repayment plan to pay a portion of the amount past due every month in addition to your regular payments until you have paid off the amount past due. These are very common foreclosure workouts, and you can usually work with the lender's loss mitigation department to arrange such a repayment plan.

Question 89: **Can I give up the property?**

Yes, you do have the option to just give up the property and negotiate a deed-in-lieu of foreclosure to avoid the costs and problems associated with foreclosure. If you do decide to take this route, be sure you have considered all other options first, such as a sale of the property, a modification of your mortgage, a refinance, or a repayment plan.

You also must be sure before you sign the deed-in-lieu of fore-closure that you will not have any deficiency in the amount still owed the bank. If you will still have a deficiency owed, the bank can still try to collect the additional funds. Be sure to work with an attorney if you are considering giving up the property to pro-tect your financial future and avoid bankruptcy.

Question 90: **How do I negotiate a deed-in-lieu of foreclosure?**

A deed-in-lieu of foreclosure is an agreement in which you voluntarily sign over all collateral in the property in exchange for release from all obligations under the mortgage. (See Question 185 for more information.) You also will lose all rights to any equity in the property that may be left over after all liens on the property are paid. Do not sign a deed-in-lieu of foreclosure unless you are certain that the lender will release you from all obligations, even if the lender cannot sell the home for enough money to cover all the money you owe the lender.

A lender will not consider a deed-in-lieu of foreclosure if it determines that you can financially afford to make your mortgage payments. To be certain that all your rights are being protected, do not try to negotiate a deed-in-lieu of foreclosure without the help of an attorney or other foreclosure professional.

Question 91: **Will the lender accept less than the debt owed on the house?**

Yes, depending upon the circumstances, but it's not easy to negotiate and you are best off hiring an attorney or foreclosure professional to assist you with the negotiation. Before a lender will even consider this option, you must be delinquent on your loan by at least two payments. Usually this does not come up in discussion until you are much closer to foreclosure.

You must prove to the lender that there is an emergency circumstance, such as a medical emergency or loss of income, which was unexpected and will not permit you to recover in the near future. The lender will also look at what other assets you have and whether you have other means to pay down a deficiency on the property upon which it plans to foreclose. You must prove to the lender that you attempted to sell the house, which does include listing it with a professional real estate salesperson, who will likely be asked for his or her assessment of market conditions that would warrant taking less than the amount owed on the house.

After all this has been considered, you may be able to negotiate a deed-in-lieu of foreclosure (see Question 90) or get the bank to accept a pre-foreclosure sale (see Question 186). If you have an FHA loan, you may also be able to ask the lender to consider a partial claim (see Question 40).

Question 92: **What is a friendly foreclosure?**

If you hear the term "friendly foreclosure," it's really only a nicer way to say "deed-in-lieu of foreclosure" (see Question 185). Sometimes if you have a friendly third party who has the means to help (such as a private investor), he or she can buy the mortgage in default and then sell the property at a foreclosure auction to clean the title of all other lien holders.

When the dust settles and the title is clean, the private investor can then sell the property back to the debtor or another predetermined person. Obviously, the person cleaning the title is a friend of the person in default on his loan, so it gets the name "friendly foreclosure."

Question 93: **Can I buy back the property after a foreclosure sale?**

Whether or not you can buy back the property after a foreclosure sale depends upon where you live and whether or not there was a clause in the mortgage or deed of trust that gives you the right to redemption. Some states do allow the right to redemption on property after it has been foreclosed on. I talk about the rules for each state in Chapter 10.

But do be careful if you are approached by someone who says he or she can rescue your home from foreclosure. Often these are scams that result in even more of a loss for you. The most common scam involves an individual or company that offers to pay off your mortgage and settle outstanding liens, provided you transfer ownership to them. You are then offered a lease arrangement with the option to buy back the home in the future.

With this type of scam you likely will be asked to pay lease payments that are so high you end up defaulting on the lease. Even if you are able to maintain the lease payments, when it comes time to buy back the property, you'll be asked to pay $50,000 to $100,000 more than the property is worth. You most likely will end up being evicted from the home at some time in the future.

Don't try to save your home without the help of an attorney who can advise you on these matters and review any contracts presented to you for possible fraud or scams.

Question 94: **Can I list the property with a real estate agent and delay foreclosure?**

Yes, in many cases you can talk with the loss mitigation department of the lender who holds your mortgage and discuss getting an extension to give you more time to sell your home. Some lenders may require you to work with a list of approved real estate agents for this purpose, whom they trust to make an honest effort to sell and who will more likely be able to get the lender to agree to a short sale, which means the lender accepts less than is due on the mortgage.

Lenders don't want to own the real estate after a foreclosure, so if the property can be sold without the need of a foreclosure, they will usually give you the time to sell as long as reasonable efforts are being made to do so. But, if the real estate agents report that you are doing things to hamper the sale, such as not keeping property in condition for it to "show" well to prospective buyers, the lender may begin foreclosure procedures.

Question 95: **Can I negotiate to stay in the property even in default?**

Yes, you should plan to stay in the property even if you are in default. If you move out of the property, the lender can determine that you have abandoned the property and start foreclosure procedures more quickly.

You don't need to move out of the property until after you have received a notice of eviction after the sale of the property. However, you should move out of the property on your own by the date set after the sale of the property to avoid additional costs for moving your things and storing them.

Question 96: **Can I reinstate my rights to the property and stop foreclosure?**

Yes, you can reinstate your rights to the property and even the mortgage as long as you have enough money to pay all past-due amounts, as well as interest, costs, and legal fees that have accumulated since you first went into default. When you reinstate your rights to the property, foreclosure will be stopped.

Even if you don't have all the money that is needed to pay all the past debt, you may be able to reinstate the mortgage by paying an agreed-upon portion of the past debt and then paying it off under a repayment plan (see Question 20). You also may be able to negotiate a mortgage modification (see Question 87) to save your home.

In both cases, you will need to prove that you now have the resources to make the payments in full and on time. The lender will ask for proof that you will have a steady source of income in the future.

Question 97: **Can I use a reverse mortgage to keep my home?**

A reverse mortgage may be an option to help you keep your home under very limited circumstances. You or your spouse must be 62 years old or older to qualify for a reverse mortgage. You also must have a substantial amount of equity built up in your home, which would be the case if you are very close to paying off the home or the value of the home has risen so quickly that your equity in the home far exceeds the mortgage.

If you meet these two criteria, it is worth considering a reverse mortgage arrangement. You can find out some basic information about reverse mortgages at AARP (*www.aarp.org/money/rev mort*). However, you should never enter into a reverse mortgage without consulting an attorney who specializes in these types of contracts to be certain that your rights to live in the property are being protected. Also, if you choose this avenue, you will not be able to leave your home to your children or other heirs.

If you do have a lot of equity in your home, you may want to consider a refinance that will stretch out your payments over a longer period of time. This would enable you to pay off the current mortgage and possibly enter into a new mortgage with lower monthly payments that you can afford. You may even be able to take out some needed cash to pay other debts.

Question 98: **Will bankruptcy stop foreclosure?**

If all else fails and you want to stop the foreclosure, bankruptcy can stop the process at least temporarily. However, the only way you will get to keep your home is if you are able to start paying the mortgage again. The mortgage is a debt secured by the property, so you can't just wipe it out.

No matter what state you live in, filing bankruptcy will give you time to think and develop a financial solution to try to keep your home. During the bankruptcy process, you will have time to start making payments so you can show in good faith that you do intend to pay the bank what is due. There are two types of bankruptcies you can consider—Chapter 7 and Chapter 13. I describe both of these in Chapter 6 of this book.

Don't be in a hurry to file bankruptcy, because you may be able to work out a repayment plan or loan modification with the lender and avoid having to add the black mark of bankruptcy to your credit report. If you also have a lot of credit card debt and want to avoid bankruptcy, you should contact a credit counselor to assist you with developing your payback plans. You can find a credit counselor near you by searching the database of the National Foundation for Credit Counseling online at *www .debtadvice.org* or you can call the foundation at (800) 388-2227.

Chapter 6

SAVING YOUR HOUSE WITH BANKRUPTCY

I f all else fails, you may be able to save your home by filing bankruptcy and restructuring your debt. While bankruptcy should not be your first line of defense to save your home, it certainly should be one tool in your arsenal, and it should be the tool of last resort. In this chapter, I review the various types of bankruptcies and explain how the process works.

Question 99: **What is bankruptcy?**

Bankruptcy is a legal process that you can use if you can't pay your bills. Through bankruptcy you can get a fresh financial start. You have the right to file bankruptcy by federal law. All bankruptcy cases are handled in a federal court.

Filing bankruptcy immediately stops all calls from creditors who are trying to collect their money. The court decides who gets paid and how much they will be paid.

The bankruptcy can eliminate the legal obligation to pay most of your unsecured debts, but it can't stop you from losing your home unless you are able to repay that debt. A bankruptcy filing can also stop the repossession of your car (at least temporarily), but that too is a secured debt and will need to be repaid if you want to keep your car. If you file bankruptcy, you can force your secured creditors to take payment over a longer period of time with lower payments.

Question 100: **How does bankruptcy stop collection efforts and foreclosures?**

When a bankruptcy is filed, the court takes control of your financial life. All creditors must work through the bankruptcy trustee to collect their money. They can no longer contact you directly. Since a bankruptcy takes at least three to four months (and often longer, depending upon how backed up the court is) to make it through the process, you have some time to get your financial ducks in a row without being hounded by creditors.

Once you file bankruptcy you can stop all foreclosures, repossessions, and wage garnishments through a special Court Order of Protection, which is executed the day you file. This is called an "automatic stay." The automatic stay protects you against all attempts to collect money from you. It will stop all bills, lawsuits, repossessions, foreclosures, and IRS liens, as well as all the calls you get from bill collectors.

Question 101: **How often can I file a bankruptcy?**

You can file for a Chapter 7 bankruptcy eight years after the discharge of a previous Chapter 7 bankruptcy or six years after the discharge of a previous Chapter 13 bankruptcy, as long as more than 70 percent of your claims were paid and the plan was proposed in good faith.

You can file a Chapter 13 bankruptcy four years after the discharge of a previous Chapter 7 bankruptcy or two years after a discharge of a previous Chapter 13 bankruptcy. You can never have two bankruptcies open or pending at the same time.

Question 102: **What is a bankruptcy trustee?**

The bankruptcy court exercises control over your financial affairs through the appointment of a person called the bankruptcy trustee. The trustee will handle your case on behalf of the bankruptcy court and will seek to assure that your unsecured creditors are paid as much as possible on the debts that you owe them. He or she also makes sure that you comply with the bankruptcy laws.

The trustee can be a local bankruptcy attorney or someone else knowledgeable about Chapter 7 or Chapter 13 bankruptcy procedures as well as the court's operations, rules, and procedures. If the trustee is not an attorney, he or she may be a businessperson who is knowledgeable about finances and personal bankruptcy.

Within days after you file your bankruptcy, you will get a Notice of Appointment of Trustee from the court. This notice will include the name, business address, and contact phone number for the trustee. The notice likely will also ask for a list of any financial documents the trustee wants to see, which can include bank statements, property appraisals, and canceled checks. The trustee will set a deadline for the submission of all requested documents as part of this notice.

Question 103: **What is Chapter 7 bankruptcy?**

When you file for a Chapter 7 bankruptcy, you ask the bankruptcy court to discharge all of your debts, which means that any unsecured credit will be wiped out to zero dollars. But, if you have secured debts, such as the mortgage on your home or loan on your car, you will have to give up your property to discharge that debt.

You also will be able to keep certain income benefits such as Social Security, unemployment compensation, veteran's benefits, public assistance, and pensions. The exemption amounts are doubled if a married couple files together.

Question 104: What are the income limits for using Chapter 7?

If your debts are primarily from consumer spending rather than spending for your business, your average monthly income must be either at or below the median income for your state in order to file for Chapter 7 bankruptcy. You can find the median income for your state at the U.S. Census Bureau Web site (*www .census.gov/hhes/income/4person.html*). Historically, 85 percent of the people who file for Chapter 7 bankruptcy fall below these income limits.

If your monthly income is higher than the state's family median income and your debts are primarily from consumer spending, you will need to take a means test.

Question 105: What is a means test?

If your current monthly income is more than your state's family median income for your family size and your debts are primarily consumer purchases, you will have to pass a financial test, called a "means test," to see if you qualify to file for Chapter 7. There are three steps you must complete to find out if you are eligible:

- Calculate your current monthly income.
- Subtract certain allowable IRS expense amounts. There are numerous charts for each type of expense published by the IRS. You can find the allowable expenses based on the size of your family for food, clothing, housekeeping supplies, personal care, transportation, utilities, and other miscellaneous expenses at *www.usdoj.gov/ust/eo/bapcpa/20061001/ meanstesting.htm*.
- Calculate your monthly projected disposable income. If the income left over after subtracting the IRS allowable expenses is $100 or more, you will need to figure out your monthly disposable income. First, you subtract all your mandatory debts for all secured credit, such as your mort-

gage and your car payments, from your monthly income. If you have more than $100 left, that is considered disposable income and will be used to repay your unsecured debt. If you can pay off 25 percent of your total unsecured debt with that disposable income, you likely would not be eligible for a Chapter 7 bankruptcy and would have to file a Chapter 13 bankruptcy instead.

Question 106: Must I use credit counseling before filing Chapter 7?

Yes, before you file for Chapter 7 bankruptcy you must work with a nonprofit credit counseling agency. The agency will determine whether or not it is feasible for you to pay off your debts outside of bankruptcy without adding to what you owe.

In order to qualify for bankruptcy, you must provide to the bankruptcy trustee for your region proof that you did receive credit counseling within a 180-day period before filing for bankruptcy. After you finish working with the agency, you will receive a certificate showing that you did participate in counseling. The agency will also give you a copy of any repayment plan worked out during the counseling. You can find out more about credit counseling and the approved agencies at the U.S. Trustee Web site (*www.usdoj.gov/ust/eo/bapcpa/ccde/index.htm*).

Question 107: Can I avoid credit counseling if I need to file quickly to stop a foreclosure?

Yes. You must certify to the bankruptcy court that you need to file to stop a foreclosure and then you must complete credit counseling within 30 days after filing. You can ask for a 15-day extension if necessary to complete the counseling.

Other exceptions to the credit counseling requirement prior to filing bankruptcy include:

- You were unable to set up an appointment with a credit counseling agency within five days after requesting it. You will need to complete the credit counseling after filing the bankruptcy, just as someone trying to stop a foreclosure must do.
- You have a physical disability that prevents you from attending counseling. However, as long as the counselor is available by phone or Internet, you won't be able to use this excuse.
- You do not have the mental capacity to understand or benefit from counseling.
- You are on active duty in a military combat zone.

Question 108: **How do I start a Chapter 7 bankruptcy?**

You can file a bankruptcy case "pro se," which means without the assistance of an attorney, but the U.S. Bankruptcy Court will make it very clear that it is extremely difficult to do so successfully. Professional advice from an attorney can help protect your rights. Bankruptcy is a very complicated legal proceeding, and you can be certain your creditors will have attorneys to question the discharge of the creditors' debt. Even if you do decide to file bankruptcy without an attorney, you should at least seek legal advice before filing to be sure you are completing the paperwork correctly and taking all the proper steps.

You can find a bankruptcy attorney through an online directory at the National Association of Consumer Bankruptcy Attorneys (*www.nacba.org*).

When setting up the appointment, check on the fees for the appointment. Many attorneys do not charge for the brief initial consultation. Bankruptcy attorneys must disclose all their fees and can only take your case after you have signed a written contract. If you can't afford to pay a bankruptcy attorney, you may be able to find free or low-cost legal services through your local or state bar association or county courthouse. You can also look under "Legal Aid" or "Legal Assistance" in the yellow pages of your phone book. If all attempts fail locally, there is a state-by-state directory at the Legal Services Corporation Web site (*www.lsc.gov*). When you get to the Web site, look for a link at the top right that says "Find Legal Assistance."

You must file your bankruptcy case in the U.S. Bankruptcy Court Division nearest to where you live. Go to the U.S. Trustee Program Web site (*www.usdoj.gov/ust/index.htm*) to find the court closest to you. At that Web site you can also find links to download all the forms you will need to file for bankruptcy.

Question 109: **What debts can be discharged in a Chapter 7 bankruptcy?**

If the court approves your bankruptcy filing under Chapter 7, the court will discharge most of your debts, including:

- Bank credit cards
- Utility bills
- Doctor and hospital bills
- Personal loans
- Department or other retail store credit cards
- Mail order and catalog purchases
- Loan balances due on loan deficiencies, such as repossessed automobiles or houses lost to foreclosure
- Most lawsuit judgments
- Obligations under leases and contracts

In order for the court to discharge this debt, you must list the debt when you file the bankruptcy. If you forget to list a debt, you will have to pay it back after the bankruptcy.

Question 110: What property is at risk in a Chapter 7 bankruptcy?

Any property secured by a mortgage, deed of trust, promissory note, or other instrument is at risk. If you are able to continue making the payments after the bankruptcy, you likely will be able to keep your home and car, as long as the court considers that property necessary. But, if you can't afford to make the payments to keep your mortgage or car loan current, the bankruptcy will not save your property; it will only delay the foreclosure until the case is completed or the court lifts the stay on the foreclosure.

Some of your other property may be exempt. Federal and state exemption systems exist to exclude some of the equity in your property. In some states the exemption amounts are higher, and you can choose to go by those amounts. In other states you can only choose to use the state exemption amounts. Anything you own with a value above the exempted amounts will be sold to pay your creditors.

Question 111: What does it cost to file a Chapter 7 bankruptcy?

The filing fee for a Chapter 7 bankruptcy is $274. If you can't afford to pay the fee, you can ask for a fee waiver or for permission to pay in installments. In addition to paying the filing fees you will also need to pay an attorney, which can range between $1,000 and $2,000. While you can file a bankruptcy case without the help of an attorney, it is definitely wise to hire one to help you through the maze of this very difficult process.

You will also need to pay the costs of copying almost all of your financial records including past tax returns, paycheck stubs, payment demands, mortgages, deeds, summonses, court judgments, credit card statements, medical bills, bank account statements, child support or alimony agreements, student loans, and any documentation of any past bankruptcies. In addition to these costs, you will need to attend at least one meeting with the bankruptcy trustee. If your creditors challenge the discharge of debts, more than one meeting may be required and you could end up with a hearing before a bankruptcy judge.

Question 112: **What is a Chapter 7 meeting of the creditors?**

As soon as your bankruptcy is filed, the court will set a date for a meeting of creditors. You must appear at this meeting, but it probably won't take place in a courtroom. Often, the meeting is held at a hearing room in the federal building at which the bankruptcy court is located. The meeting is run by the bankruptcy trustee, not by a judge.

During this meeting the bankruptcy trustee and your creditors can ask questions about the financial information included in the filing and about other issues they believe are relevant to the bankruptcy filing and your ability to pay the debt.

For example, you may be asked about expected tax refunds; recent large payments made to other creditors, family members, or friends; any documents that may be missing; and any inconsistencies in the information provided. If you aren't represented by a lawyer, you will probably face stiffer questioning about the information provided and how you calculated property exemptions.

Creditors rarely show up at these meetings. Most of the questions will come from the bankruptcy trustee. If the paperwork you submitted is complete and well prepared, the questions will be brief and the meeting quick and relatively painless.

The primary reason creditors might object is if they believe the debts you incurred were the result of a fraudulent act. For example, if you acquire a lot of debt just prior to filing for bankruptcy, that could be considered fraudulent behavior. Also, if the creditor believes you made false statements to get a loan, he or she could challenge the charge-off of the debt.

Question 113: **What key issues does the Chapter 7 bankruptcy judge decide that can affect my property?**

In most Chapter 7 bankruptcies a judge will not be involved, but if an issue is contested you will need to appear before a judge. Some key issues that can be contested include these:

- Your income level appears too high for Chapter 7 and you want to ask for an exception because of special circumstances.
- One of your creditors contests your right to file a Chapter 7 bankruptcy or discharge a particular debt.
- You want to ask a judge to discharge a debt that is not normally discharged in a Chapter 7 bankruptcy, such as a student loan or past-due taxes.
- You want to eliminate a lien on your property that would otherwise survive (remain against your property) a bankruptcy without a ruling from a judge. To get rid of that type of lien the judge would have to order it specifically.
- You are handling your own bankruptcy without the help of an attorney and want to keep making payments on your car or home. This is called reaffirming the debt.

Question 114: **How does a Chapter 7 bankruptcy case end?**

Your Chapter 7 bankruptcy will end with the discharge of all debts that are eligible to be discharged. When your debt is discharged, your creditor can never try to collect it from you again or report it to a credit bureau as an ongoing debt. Your credit report will likely show the debt as discharged by bankruptcy, but the creditor cannot indicate that you still owe the money or are past due on payments.

You can also decide to change your mind before the debt is discharged and withdraw your bankruptcy filing. In most cases the court will do so without a problem, unless your withdrawal is not in the best interest of your creditors. The trustee may oppose the withdrawal of your case if your nonexempt assets could be sold to pay your creditors.

If you do decide to withdraw your case, you can file again later, but you may have to wait at least 180 days to do so, and pay a new filing fee. You also have the option of converting your case into another type of bankruptcy, such as a Chapter 13 (discussed in Question 117), which people sometimes do to save property that may otherwise be sold to pay creditors.

Question 115: **What is Chapter 11 bankruptcy?**

A Chapter 11 bankruptcy is primarily used by businesses so they can stop their creditors from collecting and have time to reorganize their debts. Individuals who consider Chapter 11 bankruptcy have assets above one or both of the Chapter 13 bankruptcy limits: Their unsecured debts exceed $307,675 or their secured debts exceed $922,975 or both are true.

At $839, it's much more expensive to file for a Chapter 11 bankruptcy. In addition, there are fees that must be paid quarterly throughout the time the court is managing your debt payment. Fees charged by the court differ depending on the amount of the disbursements. For example, if the disbursements total less than $15,000, the quarterly fee would be $250. The fee can be as high as $10,000 per quarter if disbursements exceed $5 million.

You will need a lawyer to file a Chapter 11 bankruptcy. These bankruptcies take much longer and are much more expensive than Chapter 7 and Chapter 13 bankruptcies because it is more likely that creditors will hire attorneys to represent them before court to question any discharge of debt.

Question 116: What is Chapter 12 bankruptcy?

Chapter 12 bankruptcy is very similar to Chapter 13 bankruptcy. The key difference is that 80 percent of the debt must come from operating a family farm. The fee for filing a Chapter 12 bankruptcy is $230.

You definitely want the help of an attorney familiar with the laws specific to Chapter 12 bankruptcy filing and who can best help you protect your property and possibly save your farm with a restructuring of your debt.

Question 117: What is Chapter 13 bankruptcy?

When you file a Chapter 13 bankruptcy, you must show how you will pay off some of your past-due and current debts over three to five years. You will be allowed to keep your most valuable property, especially your home and car. In most cases, the payments you will be required to make are at least as much as the regular monthly payments on your mortgage and car loan, with some extra payments to get caught up on the amount that is past due.

A Chapter 13 bankruptcy can help you save valuable property that is not exempt, as long as you can afford to pay creditors from your income, and provided you are given some extra time to pay. You must have enough income to pay for your necessities and to keep up with the required payments as they come due. The bankruptcy court will set a monthly payment that you make to the trustee. The trustee then will make the required payments to your creditors.

Question 118: How do I start a Chapter 13 bankruptcy?

You start a Chapter 13 bankruptcy by filling out a package of forms very similar to those you must complete for a Chapter 7 bankruptcy. You can find the forms you need and download them at the U.S. Trustee Program Web site (*www.usdoj.gov/ust/ index.htm*).

The key differences between a Chapter 7 and a Chapter 13 bankruptcy is that in addition to the forms you must complete for a Chapter 7 bankruptcy, you must also:

- Prepare a workable plan to repay some or all of your debts during the plan period, which can be either three or five years, depending on your income. If your income is below the state's median income, you can submit a three-year plan. If it's above the state's median income, you must submit a five-year plan. Some creditors must receive 100 percent of what you owe them, while others receive a smaller percentage or possibly nothing at all if you won't have enough disposable income left to pay them after the mandatory debts are paid, such as your mortgage, car payment, or child support.
- Prove that you've filed your federal and state income tax returns for the previous four years.
- Submit your income tax return for the previous year.

To successfully complete your three- or five-year plan, you must make all the payments required by the bankruptcy trustee.

Question 119: **What is a repayment plan?**

A repayment plan is the plan that you propose when you file for Chapter 13. You submit the plan to the bankruptcy trustee, who can amend it after he reviews it. He can either agree to what you submit or change it after receiving any additional information he may request. To discharge remaining debts that will not be paid during the period of time you are in a repayment plan, you must make all payments required by your plan. In addition to making all payments, to successfully complete a Chapter 13 repayment plan you must:

- Be current on your federal and state income taxes.
- Remain current on any child support or alimony obligations.
- File your annual federal income tax return with the court.
- File an annual income and expense statement with the court.

You also must provide your creditors with the copies of the income tax returns you file with the court, if they request a copy.

Once you've completed your three-year or five-year plan, the court will discharge all remaining unpaid debt unless a creditor challenges the discharge of the debt. A judge would then have to look at the facts and determine whether or not the debt can be discharged. In most cases credit card bills, medical bills, and legal debts can be discharged, as can most court judgments and loans. You cannot ask to discharge court-imposed fines, back child support and alimony, student loans, recent back taxes, unfiled taxes, or debts that you incurred from a civil judgment that arose after your willful or malicious acts, such as causing injury or death from drunk driving. Debts that you cannot discharge will survive the bankruptcy, and you will still be obligated to pay them.

Question 120: What property is at risk in a Chapter 13 bankruptcy?

All property secured by a mortgage, deed of trust, or promissory note is at risk if you can't continue to make the required payments. Otherwise, you are not required to give up property that you own in Chapter 13 as you would in Chapter 7. The court will not force the sale of property to pay your unsecured debts.

You will be able to keep your house and car as long as you can stay current on your payments. As part of your payment plan, you can also pay off any past-due amounts, as well as interest and legal fees incurred. Chapter 13 is the remedy of choice if you are facing foreclosure on your home.

Question 121: What are the costs of filing a Chapter 13 bankruptcy?

The cost of filing for a Chapter 13 bankruptcy is $189. If you can't afford the fee you can apply for a waiver of the fee. You are best off seeking legal advice when filing for bankruptcy, but that can get very expensive with a Chapter 13. Legal costs for a Chapter 13 bankruptcy usually range between $2,500 and $4,000. An attorney who knows the bankruptcy law can help you protect your rights and can work with you to get the best repayment arrangement and save your property.

Though it isn't recommended, you can decide to handle the case on your own to save money, but you will still need to pay for some services. You definitely should get some self-help law books. You also should plan to seek some legal help by telephone as you prepare the paperwork, which usually costs about $100 an hour. In addition, to ensure that you properly complete the bankruptcy filing forms, you should seek help from someone who specializes in bankruptcy petition preparation, which can range from $300 to $600.

Question 122: What is a Chapter 13 meeting of the creditors?

Usually about a month after you file your Chapter 13 bankruptcy petition, the court will schedule a meeting of the creditors. Once this is scheduled, the court will send an official notice of the bankruptcy filing and the meeting to you and all your creditors. The trustee will also make sure you've filed and paid your taxes for the past four years. If you haven't, he'll put off the meeting to give you time to complete your taxes. You can't proceed with a Chapter 13 repayment plan without your tax filings being up-to-date.

In most cases these meetings last only about 15 minutes, provided you filed complete and accurate information. The bankruptcy trustee will lead the meeting and will ask most of the questions. There will not be a judge at this meeting.

The primary purpose of the meeting will be to review your repayment plan for its fairness and its legality, as well as your ability to make the payments you proposed.

The trustee does have a vested interest in your success because he gets a percentage of all payments doled out to creditors as part of your repayment plan. The trustee probably will ask most of the questions, but your creditors may question certain aspects of your repayment plan if they don't think the plan is reasonable. The unsecured creditors, who likely will get very little under the plan, may question your calculation of disposable income and push for an increase of that disposable income.

Expect to find upset creditors at the meeting. You may even need to modify the plan to appease them, and resubmit the plan prior to your confirmation hearing before the judge.

Question 123: **What are the key issues a judge decides in a Chapter 13 bankruptcy that can affect my property?**

All Chapter 13 filers must make at least one appearance before a bankruptcy judge. This is called the confirmation hearing. The judge can either confirm your proposed repayment plan or reject it and ask you to make changes. Most times, if the plan is rejected, it will be because you don't have enough disposable income to pay your priority creditors and stay current on your secured debts. You can continue to modify the plan until the judge approves it or decides it is hopeless. Each time you amend the plan, you must go through another confirmation hearing.

A judge can rule on the value of an asset (if the creditor believes it's worth more than you think it's worth); on a creditor or trustee's objection to parts of your plan; and on whether or not a debt should be discharged if questioned by a creditor. The judge also can eliminate a lien on your property or decide that it will survive bankruptcy. In addition, he or she can reaffirm a contract, such as your mortgage, so you can keep your home. If the judge rules that Chapter 13 is hopeless, you can switch to a Chapter 7 bankruptcy, but you won't be able to keep your house unless you can make the mortgage payments.

Question 124: **How does a Chapter 13 bankruptcy case end?**

A Chapter 13 case ends when you complete your repayment plan in three to five years, are current on your income tax returns, are current on your child support or alimony payments, and complete a budget management course approved by the trustee. Any remaining debt that qualifies will be wiped out. Any remaining debt that doesn't qualify to be wiped out will still need to be paid.

You will need to live strictly within your means throughout the entire time of the repayment period. The trustee will not allow you to spend money on anything he or she deems nonessential.

You can't get the benefits of discharge until you successfully complete the repayment plan. If you don't succeed, you may be able to file for Chapter 7 bankruptcy. Historically only about 35 percent of Chapter 13 filers make it to the end and get their remaining debts discharged.

Question 125: **What happens if my Chapter 13 repayment plan fails?**

If you can't complete the plan on time, you can ask for further modification of the plan. As long as you continue to show good faith that you want to be responsible, the court will consider modifications to the repayment plan. You will need to keep the trustee on your side. He or she will be the one that the judge will look to when considering modifications and deciding whether or not to confirm the modified plan.

If you can't continue to make payments into your plan for reasons beyond your control, such as job loss or medical emergency, a judge might let you end your case early and discharge the remaining debt on the basis of hardship. If you can't get a hardship discharge, you can file for Chapter 7 bankruptcy.

If you do end up filing a Chapter 7 bankruptcy, all the money you paid into the Chapter 13 repayment plan will be for nothing. The judge also has the option to dismiss your case, meaning that you will owe all the debt you did before filing for bankruptcy.

Question 126: **How do I determine which bankruptcy is right for me?**

If your income is higher than the state's median family income, you won't have a choice to make. You will have to file Chapter 13, unless most of the outstanding debt is related to your business. If it's mostly business debt, you can choose to file a Chapter 11 bankruptcy. If your debt is primarily from your family farm, you can choose to file Chapter 12.

Otherwise, you probably will want to file Chapter 7, which allows your debt to be discharged without having to pay any of your unsecured debt. Chapter 7 is faster and easier to file and you don't have to make any payments over time. In most cases a Chapter 7 case can be opened and closed in three to six months. You emerge debt free except for mortgage and car loans, plus any other debt that is not eligible for a discharge.

Historically, few Chapter 7 filers have lost any property, because state and federal exemption rules allow them to keep most necessities. However, the new bankruptcy law that passed in October 2005 might make it harder for people to keep all their property with a Chapter 7 bankruptcy. Under the new law, property must be valued at its replacement value, which could make it harder to meet the limits set in the exemption rules.

Question 127: **What are secured debts?**

A secured debt is any debt in which you stand to lose the property if you don't make the payments. Most secured debts are created when you sign loan papers that give the creditor a security interest in your property. The most common secured debts include:

- Mortgages
- Home equity loans (second mortgages)
- Loans for cars, boats, tractors, motorcycles, or recreation vehicles
- Store charges with a security agreement. Most credit cards are unsecured, but certain stores do require you to sign a security agreement for purchases. Sears and JC Penney are two stores that require security agreements when you use their charge card.
- Personal loans from banks, credit unions, or finance companies—if the financial institution required you to put up collateral when you signed the loan agreement.
- Judicial liens
- Statutory liens
- Tax liens

To review the various types of liens and their impact on your property, read Chapter 3.

Question 128: **What is personal liability?**

Whenever you take on a debt, you have a personal liability to repay that debt. This means you are obligated to the creditor to repay the money due. When you file bankruptcy, you can have all or part of the personal liability wiped out. If successful in wiping out that liability as part of a bankruptcy, the creditor cannot sue you to collect the debt.

Question 129: **What is security interest?**

A security interest is a creditor's legal claim on the property that you are using to borrow the funds you need, whether it's to buy a house, a car, or some other major purchase. The security interest becomes a lien on the property, which the creditor can use to repossess the property in question.

A security interest lien cannot be wiped out with a bankruptcy. You still must pay the money due, or the property can be repossessed. A bankruptcy court cannot wipe out a debt if the creditor holds a security interest in the property.

Question 130: **What does it mean to redeem the property during bankruptcy?**

While you file bankruptcy, you have the right to "redeem" or buy back the property from the creditor rather than allow the creditor to take the property and sell it to someone else. For example, if you own a house or car that has a replacement value that is lower than the amount of debt you owe on the property, you can buy back the property at its replacement value rather than pay off the full amount of the debt.

You can redeem the property by using cash you received after your bankruptcy filing date from friends or family. You also can sell some of your property that is exempt under the bankruptcy rules and then use the cash to redeem other property that you lost.

If you can't raise the cash to redeem the property with a lump sum, you may want to consider a Chapter 13 bankruptcy, in which you can pay off the property's replacement value as part of your repayment plan.

Question 131: **What does it mean to reaffirm the debt during bankruptcy?**

When you reaffirm a debt during bankruptcy, it means that you and the creditor write up a new agreement that sets out the amount you owe and the terms of repayment of the debt. This essentially becomes a brand-new debt. You may even be able to work out better terms than you had in your original loan agreement.

By reaffirming the debt you get to keep the property as long as you make the required payments as set out in the new loan agreement. When you reaffirm a debt, both the creditor's lien on the property that you used as collateral and your personal liability will survive the bankruptcy intact.

If you do reaffirm a debt as part of the bankruptcy agreement, there is no way you will be able to walk away from the debt after your bankruptcy. You should only reaffirm a debt on property if it's the only way to keep it and you know you will be able to make the payments.

Question 132: **What is a "Statement of Intention" when filing bankruptcy?**

A Statement of Intention is a document you must file with your bankruptcy package that tells your secured creditors what you plan to do with the collateral that is secured. For each piece of property that is used as collateral, you must state whether you plan to surrender the property, redeem it, or reaffirm it.

If you fail to file the Statement of Intention within 30 days after you file your initial bankruptcy petition, the court will lift the automatic stay on the property and you will be in default of your security agreement. The creditor will then have the right to repossess the property and sell it at a public auction or by other means permitted by law in your state.

The automatic stay will also be lifted if you fail to carry out what you state in the Statement of Intentions. The deadline for completing your stated intentions is unclear in the new bankruptcy law, but the longest you will have is 45 days after the first meeting of the creditors. To be safe, start working with your creditors immediately if you want to keep the property and avoid repossession or foreclosure.

Question 133: **What is an automatic stay?**

An automatic stay goes into effect immediately after you file for bankruptcy. This stay prohibits creditors and collection agencies from taking any action to collect the money you owe them. Sometimes a creditor will file a motion to lift the stay. Others may begin collection proceedings without seeking permission from the court.

Under the new bankruptcy law, the court is more likely to give creditors permission to continue trying to collect, but for most types of debt, creditors are stopped in their tracks from making harassing calls to collect debt, sending threatening attorney's letters, or filing a lawsuit seeking a monetary judgment.

Companies collecting debts owed to credit card companies, medical debts, attorney's fees, debts arising from breach of contract, and legal judgments other than child support or alimony will be stopped by the automatic stay.

Domestic relations proceedings, evictions (obtained prior to bankruptcy filing), and many tax proceedings are not stopped by the automatic stay. Foreclosures on a home cannot be stopped if you filed another bankruptcy in the previous two years and that court lifted the stay in that proceeding. Utility companies cannot turn off your utilities when the automatic stay is first put in place, but you must give the utility company at least a deposit toward payments within 20 days or some other means to assure that you will make future payments to keep your utilities on.

Question 134: **What is my bankruptcy estate?**

Any property you own on the day you file your bankruptcy is considered your bankruptcy estate. This includes all property you possess. That means anything you own, even if you still owe money on it.

Property that you have in possession but that belongs to someone else will not be part of your bankruptcy estate, but property you own that is in someone else's possession will be part of it. You also must consider property you are entitled to receive as of your bankruptcy filing date, but haven't yet gotten. This property also will be part of your bankruptcy estate, and can include wages, royalties, commissions, tax refunds, vacation or termination pay, inherited property, insurance proceeds, and money owed to you.

Question 135: **What is community property?**

If you live in a community property state, all property owned by you or your spouse that was acquired during marriage is usually considered "community property" and is owned by both spouses. States with community property laws include Arizona, Idaho, Louisiana, Nevada, New Mexico, Texas, Washington, and Wisconsin.

When you file bankruptcy jointly with your spouse in a community property state, all of the property you own jointly as community property, as well as all the property you own separately, becomes part of the bankruptcy estate. If you file bankruptcy, but your spouse doesn't, all your separate property plus all your community property becomes part of the bankruptcy estate.

Question 136: What is marital property in a common-law property state?

In a common-law property state, which includes all states not listed as community property states, any property acquired by a married person during marriage is the property of that person separately, unless the person agrees with his or her spouse to hold the property jointly. If you live in a common-law property state and file bankruptcy jointly, all the property you own either together or separately becomes part of the bankruptcy estate. If you file for bankruptcy alone, only your separate property and half of your property owned jointly becomes part of the bankruptcy estate.

Question 137: How is property held under a "tenancy by the entirety" handled in bankruptcy?

Property held by you and your spouse as tenants by the entirety will be handled differently depending upon the state you live in. If you live in Delaware, the District of Columbia, Florida, Hawaii, Illinois, Indiana, Maryland, Massachusetts, Michigan, Missouri, North Carolina, Pennsylvania, Tennessee, Vermont, Virginia, or Wyoming, and only one spouse files for bankruptcy, the bankruptcy court and creditors usually cannot take the property that both spouses own as tenants by the entirety. If you file jointly, the property will become part of the bankruptcy estate. If you own property as tenants by the entirety, discuss this with your attorney before filing for bankruptcy.

Question 138: What are property exemptions?

The primary purpose of bankruptcy is to give debtors a fresh financial start, so you will not be left completely destitute. You can keep certain property, which will be tagged as exempt property. Neither the bankruptcy trustee nor your creditors can take exempt property as part of their collection efforts. How much of your property will be exempt depends upon the state you live in.

For example, the federal exemption system allows you to keep $18,450 of equity in your home; $2,950 of equity in your car; $475 per item in household goods up to a total of $9,850; $1,850 in things you need for your job; $975 in any property, plus up to $9,250 of any unused exemption in your home. In some states the exemption amounts are higher, and you can choose to go by those amounts rather than the federal amounts. In some states you can only go by the state exemption amounts. Anything you own above the exempted amounts will be sold to pay your creditors if you file Chapter 7 bankruptcy. If you successfully complete a Chapter 13 bankruptcy, your property will not be at risk.

Question 139: What are state exemption systems?

While Congress established federal exemption as part of the bankruptcy law, most states prefer to set their own exemption rules. In fact, every state has its own list of exempt property. Exemptions allow you to keep certain property outside of the bankruptcy filing.

Exemption systems allow you to keep the things you need to live day-to-day. Used household goods and personal effects have little resale value, so they do not offer a good resale value for creditors and are exempt. You can find out what is exempt in your state at *http://www.bankruptcyinformation.com/services .html*. Some states allow you to choose whether you want to use the state or federal exemptions. States that offer this choice include Arkansas, Connecticut, Hawaii, Massachusetts, Michigan, Minnesota, New Hampshire, New Jersey, New Mexico, Pennsylvania, Rhode Island, Texas, Vermont, Washington, and Wisconsin.

Question 140: **How do exemptions work?**

Whether you use the federal exemptions or your state exemptions, the exemption amount indicates the amount of equity in a particular type of property that you can keep. For example, in some states all home furnishings, wedding rings, and clothing are exempt without regard to value. In some states, you can keep your home no matter how much equity you have in it, but in most states a specific home equity exemption exists. (Equity simply means value above what you owe in debt on that property.)

When there is a dollar limit stated, any equity in your property over that amount becomes nonexempt property. The property would have to be sold and you would get to keep the dollar amount of the exemption. In addition to these exemptions, states also have a homestead exemption, which I explain in Question 143.

A trustee will not take the property if the value of the nonexempt portion, after costs of storage and sale are deducted, is not high enough to make it worthwhile to take it. For example, if your used furniture exceeds the allowable state exemption but not by enough to get significant funds to pay creditors, the bankruptcy trustee probably will not take it.

Question 141: **What are residency requirements for exemption claims?**

In an effort to prevent gaming the bankruptcy system, such as moving to a state with better exemptions before filing for bankruptcy, Congress requires that you live in your state for at least two years in order to file according to that state's exemption system. If you live in your current state for more than 91 days but less than two years, you must file according to the exemption system of the state in which you lived for most of the 180 days immediately prior to the two-year period before filing for bankruptcy.

If you haven't lived in your current state for at least 91 days, you will have to wait until you have lived there for 91 days before you can file for bankruptcy and use state bankruptcy exemption rules. If you are living in a state that allows you to use the federal exemption system, it doesn't matter how long you have lived in that state as long as you choose to use the federal system. If you're in a situation in which there are no state exemptions, you can use the federal exemption system.

Homestead exemption rules are even stiffer. If you bought your home in your current state less than 40 months before your filing date, your homestead exemption may be subject to a $125,000 cap no matter which state exemption system you use. Prior to these residency requirements, people could move to a state with an unlimited homestead value exemption, qualify for the state's homestead exemption, and then file for bankruptcy and have all equity in their home exempt, which could be in the millions. Now you have to live in the new state for at least 40 months before being able to take advantage of more generous homestead exemptions.

Question 142: **What are federal bankruptcy code exemptions?**

If for some reason your residency puts you in a situation in which you are not eligible to use any state exemptions, or if you live in Arkansas, Connecticut, Hawaii, Massachusetts, Michigan, Minnesota, New Hampshire, New Jersey, New Mexico, Pennsylvania, Rhode Island, Texas, Vermont, Washington, or Wisconsin, you can use the federal bankruptcy code exemptions.

These include:

- Homestead exemption of $18,450, which includes a co-op or mobile home and a burial plot. If you don't use all of this exemption, you can apply up to $9,250 of the unused portion to other property.

- All disability, illness, or unemployment benefits.
- All life insurance payments for a person that you were dependent upon for support.
- All alimony and child support payments needed for support.
- All ERISA-qualified benefits needed for support, including IRAs.
- All animals, crops, clothing, appliances, books, furnishings, household goods, and musical instruments, up to $475 per item, for a total of $9,850.
- All health aids.
- All lost earnings payments.
- All personal injury recoveries up to $17,425 (not including pain and suffering or financial loss).
- All wrongful death recoveries for a person you depended upon.
- All crime victim compensation.
- All public assistance.
- All Social Security.
- All unemployment compensation.
- All veteran's benefits.
- All items you need as tools of your trade up to $1,850.
- Up to $875 of any property plus up to $9,250 of unused homestead exemption.

Question 143: **What are homestead exemptions?**

A homestead exemption is a special exemption from the bankruptcy code that protects your primary residence. Homestead exemption laws do not protect second homes, vacation homes, or other real estate property that you are not living in when you file for bankruptcy.

There are several different types of exemptions. The District of Columbia has an unlimited homestead exemption. The states of Arkansas, Florida, Iowa, Kansas, Oklahoma, South Dakota, and Texas have homestead exemptions based on lot size only. Alabama, Hawaii, Louisiana, Michigan, Minnesota, Mississippi, Nebraska, and Oregon based their homestead exemption on lot size and equity. Delaware, Maryland, New Jersey, and Pennsylvania offer no homestead exemption from bankruptcy. All states not mentioned offer a homestead exemption based on equity only.

Question 144: Can I get an unlimited homestead exemption?

The only place you can live and get an unlimited homestead exemption is the District of Columbia. However, the states that offer homestead exemption on lot size only do give you a lot of leeway. Those states include Arkansas, Florida, Iowa, Kansas, Oklahoma, South Dakota, and Texas.

Question 145: Which states base their exemption on lot size, and how does that work?

In states that offer a homestead exemption based solely on lot size, your personal residence is exempt from bankruptcy provided the lot it sits on is no larger than the maximum allowed.

Texas has an unlimited homestead exemption provided your property does not exceed a lot size of 10 acres in a town, village, or city, or 100 acres (200 acres for families) elsewhere in the state. In Florida, you can get an unlimited homestead exemption on real or personal property including a mobile or other type of modular home provided your property does not exceed ½ acre in a municipality or 160 acres elsewhere in the state.

In Arkansas, you can get an unlimited exemption if your property is ¼ acre or less in a city, town, or village, or 80 acres elsewhere. Iowa offers a homestead exemption for real property or an apartment to an unlimited value as long as the property does not exceed ½ acre in a town or city or 40 acres elsewhere.

Kansas has an unlimited exemption on value of the property as long as it does not exceed 1 acre in a town or city or 160 acres on a farm. To get an unlimited homestead exemption in South Dakota, your property cannot exceed 1 acre in town or 160 acres elsewhere.

In Oklahoma, you can get an unlimited exemption for real property or a manufactured home as long as the property does not exceed a quarter acre in a city, town, or village or 160 acres elsewhere.

Question 146: Which states base their exemption on lot size and equity, and how does that work?

In states that offer homestead exemption from bankruptcy based on lot size and equity, both factors are taken into consideration when calculating your exemption.

For example, Alabama allows you to exempt up to $5,000 of equity, and the property cannot exceed 100 acres. Hawaii allows a $30,000 homestead exemption to a head of family over age 65 and $20,000 to all others as long as the property does not exceed 1 acre. Louisiana allows a $25,000 homestead exemption as long as it does not exceed 5 acres in a city or town or 200 acres elsewhere. Louisiana does allow an exemption for the full value of your homestead property if your debt is the result of a catastrophic or terminal illness or injury, provided that you owned the property at least one year before filing.

Michigan allows up to a $3,500 homestead exemption as long as the property does not exceed one lot in a town, village, or city, or 40 acres elsewhere.

Minnesota allows a homestead exemption of $200,000 ($500,000 if the property is used for agricultural purposes). The property cannot exceed ½ acre in a city or 160 acres elsewhere. Mississippi allows a homestead exemption of up to $75,000 on property you own provided it does not exist on a lot over 160 acres. In order for a mobile home to qualify, you must own the land on which it is located. Nebraska allows a homestead exemption of $12,500 provided you own property that does not exceed two lots in a city or village or 160 acres elsewhere. Oregon allows homestead exemptions based on the type of home—for example, $25,000 ($33,000 for joint owners) for real property; $23,000 ($30,000 for joint owners) for mobile homes on land you own; or $20,000 ($27,000 for joint owners) on land you don't own. The property cannot exceed one block in a town or city or 160 acres elsewhere.

Question 147: **Which states base their exemptions on equity only, and how does that work?**

States that base their exemptions solely on equity set a dollar limit for that equity. If the amount of equity exceeds the allowable exemption, the property will be sold to pay the debtors. You will receive cash in the amount allowed by the homestead exemption, which you can use for anything you choose.

States that offer a homestead exemption based solely on equity include Alaska, Arizona, California, Colorado, Idaho, Illinois, Indiana, Kentucky, Maine, Massachusetts, Missouri, Montana, Nevada, New Hampshire, New Mexico, New York, North Carolina, North Dakota, Ohio, Rhode Island, South Carolina, Tennessee, Utah, Vermont, Virginia, Washington, West Virginia, Wisconsin, and Wyoming.

Question 148: **Which states do not offer any homestead exemptions?**

Four states offer no homestead exemptions—Delaware, Maryland, New Jersey, and Pennsylvania. In all four states, if property is held as tenancy by the entirety, the property may be exempt against debts owed by only one spouse. I explain tenancy by the entirety in Question 137.

Question 149: **What do homestead exemptions protect?**

Homestead exemptions protect the equity you have in the property. You must reside in the home as your primary residence when you file for bankruptcy in order to claim a homestead exemption. You cannot use a homestead exemption to protect a second home, a vacation home, or any other real estate you own. In most states, homestead exemptions can apply to mobile homes and boats, if that is what you use as your primary residence.

Question 150: **What is a declaration of homestead, and what states require it?**

In many states the homestead exemption automatically kicks in when you file for bankruptcy, but in some states you must file a "Declaration of Homestead" with the county in which the residence is located in order to use that state's homestead exemption. States that require you to file a Declaration of Homestead include Alabama, Idaho, Massachusetts, Montana, Nevada, Texas, Utah, Virginia, and Washington.

Question 151: **What is a "wildcard" exemption?**

Some states allow you to increase the amount of your homestead exemption with a state wildcard exemption. This exemption allows you to add a dollar value in equity to any property that you choose to use it on. Federal exemptions also allow a wildcard exemption. A federal wildcard exemption allows you an additional $975 in exemptions. State exemptions vary from $300 for Pennsylvania to as high as $8,000 in New Hampshire.

States that allow wildcard exemptions to apply to real estate owned include California, Connecticut, Georgia, Indiana, Kentucky, Maine, Maryland, Missouri, Ohio, Vermont, Virginia (available only if you are a disabled veteran), and West Virginia. Some states do offer a wildcard exemption that can be used to protect other property, but cannot be used as an addition to the homestead exemption.

Question 152: **How long ago must I have acquired my home to use my state's homestead exemption?**

You must have acquired your home at least 40 months previously to use your state's homestead exemption without any restrictions. If you bought your home within 40 months (3 years 4 months) of filing, but purchased that new home in the same state with proceeds from *another* home that you owned in that state at least 40 months prior to filing bankruptcy, then you can use your state's homestead exemption without any restrictions as well.

If you bought your home within 40 months of filing and have lived in your state two or more years, you can use that state's exemption, but it will be subject to a homestead exemption cap of $125,000. If you have lived in your state for less than two years before filing, you must use the homestead exemption available in the state where you were living for the better part of a 180-day period prior to the two-year period, and what you do use as a homestead exemption will be capped at $125,000.

Some believe that the residency requirements will be declared unconstitutional because they impose a burden on filers' fundamental right to travel. If you are limited by these residency requirements, be certain to check with an attorney regarding any cases questioning the constitutionality of this clause.

Question 153: **What if I bought a new home too recently to use my state's exemption, but I owned a home in the same state previously?**

As long as you owned a home in the same state at least 40 months prior to your filing bankruptcy and you use the proceeds from the sale of that home that you owned previously, you will be able to use your state's homestead exemption. If you bought your home within the 40 months before filing and lived in your state for two or more years, you can use your state's homestead exemption, but it will be subject to a $125,000 cap.

Question 154: **What happens to my exemption if I live in the state less than two years?**

If you live in the state less than two years before filing, you must use the homestead exemption available in the state where you were living for the better part of the 180-day period prior to the two-year period, and it will be subject to a $125,000 cap. You can use the federal homestead exemption instead if your state permits that choice, or if for some reason you are in a limbo of having no state to use.

Question 155: **Can my homestead exemption be capped for criminal or deceptive actions?**

If you have committed a felony, a securities violation, or certain other crimes or intentional torts that led to the death or serious bodily injury of another person, your homestead exemption may be capped at $125,000, but that will be at the discretion of the bankruptcy court. The court may lift the cap if it finds that the homestead in question is needed to support you and your dependents. The court could also limit your homestead exemption if you tried to cheat your creditors.

Question 156: **If I don't have any equity in my home, can I keep the home if I file a Chapter 7 bankruptcy?**

You will be able to keep your home if you have no equity in the home and file a Chapter 7 bankruptcy, provided you continue to keep your mortgage payments current. If you have no equity in your home, the bankruptcy trustee won't get any money from selling your home, so there are no proceeds that can be used to pay your creditors.

However, if you don't pay off any security liens that may exist on the property, which includes a mortgage, deed of trust, or tax lien, the lender or government still has the right to foreclose on your property.

Question 157: **If I do have some equity in my home, can I keep the home if I file a Chapter 7 bankruptcy?**

If the difference between the market value of your home and the debt you secured against that home is less than the homestead exemption in your state, then you likely will be able to keep your home as long as you stay current on the payments. The bankruptcy trustee will get nothing out of selling your home that he or she can use to pay the creditors, and won't get any commission from the sale.

Even if your equity is slightly above what is allowed by the homestead exemption rule, the trustee will need to consider the cost of sale, which is usually about 10 percent above the sale price, and decide whether it is financially worth forcing the sale.

Question 158: **Can I have too much equity in my home to keep the home when I file a Chapter 7 bankruptcy?**

Yes. If the difference between the market value of your home and the total debt that you have secured against that home is considerably more than the homestead exemption, you are at risk of losing that home. If the bankruptcy trustee believes that he or she can sell that home, pay the sales costs, give you the amount of the homestead exemption in cash, and still have significant funds leftover to pay off your creditors, he or she will force the sale of your home.

If any money is left after the trustee gets his or her cut, your creditors are paid in full, and you receive the cash to cover your homestead exemption, the leftover funds go to you.

Question 159: **If I have too much equity in my home to keep it when I file Chapter 7, is there an alternative to losing my home?**

If you have too much equity in your home to keep it if you file Chapter 7, you may be able to refinance your mortgage or take out a home equity loan or line of credit to pay off your creditors and save your home. Another alternative to save your home without taking out a new loan would be to raise enough cash from family or friends or by selling other exempt property to satisfy the bankruptcy trustee.

Question 160: **Is Chapter 13 bankruptcy a better alternative if I have a lot of equity in my home?**

Yes, a Chapter 13 bankruptcy is a better alternative if you have a lot of equity and want to save your home. The Chapter 13 bankruptcy will enable you to set up a repayment plan to cover your debts. The repayment must be completed in three to five years. Chapter 13 lets you pay your debts out of your income over time rather than force the sale of your property. I discuss Chapter 13 bankruptcies and how they work beginning with Question 117.

Question 161: **Can I use Chapter 13 to buy time?**

Yes, some people decide to file a Chapter 13 bankruptcy to stop foreclosure proceedings and buy time to sell their home on their own terms. Since Chapter 13 involves setting up a three- or five-year repayment plan, you can use the time it takes to set up that plan and possibly begin making payments to get your financial house in order.

This can be particularly useful if your financial difficulties are due to a job loss, and you just got a new job and expect to be able to get yourself back on your feet. If things don't work out, you can always file a Chapter 7 in the future, but you will have bought some additional time to raise the needed funds to keep your house.

Question 162: Is there a waiting period from the time I refinance to the time I can file for bankruptcy?

If you decide that you want to try to keep your house or you want to reduce the equity in your home so you can use your state's homestead exemption to protect your home, you can do that with a refinance or an equity loan. You will have to wait 90 days before filing for bankruptcy after you start making payments on a new loan.

You also must be careful about who you pay money to in the 90 days before filing for bankruptcy. If you pay $600 or more to a creditor in the 90 days before filing, that payment can be set aside by the bankruptcy trustee as a forbidden "preferential payment to a creditor." There is an exception if the payments are part of the normal course of business or for the necessities of life, such as housing, utilities, and food. Also, if you pay $600 or more to a friend or relative in the year before filing, these payments can be set aside by the bankruptcy trustee.

Question 163: If I'm behind in my mortgage payments on my home, can a bankruptcy protect me?

No, a bankruptcy will not protect you if you are behind on your mortgage payments on your home. However, a Chapter 13 bankruptcy may help you reorganize your debt so you can buy time to catch up on your past-due amounts.

A Chapter 7 bankruptcy may be able to help you if you can get through the process fast enough and fend off foreclosure. After the bankruptcy case and after you've wiped out your other debt, you may have enough money to get your mortgage payments up-to-date after most of your unsecured debt is discharged and you no longer have to make payments on that debt. If you do plan to use this tactic, be sure to work with your lender's loss mitigation department to set up a temporary modification of your mortgage loan (discussed in Question 39) or a repayment plan (discussed in Question 88).

Question 164: Can liens on my property be eliminated in a Chapter 7 bankruptcy?

You cannot remove a consensual lien (see Question 60 for an explanation of consensual liens) on your property through a Chapter 7 bankruptcy. You can remove most judicial liens against exempt property, including property that is protected by a homestead exemption. While you can remove a homeowner's association lien filed prior to a bankruptcy, any fees due after the bankruptcy will have to be paid.

Question 165: Can I use bankruptcy to get rid of a judicial lien on my property?

Yes, you can use bankruptcy to remove a judicial lien placed on your property because of a civil lawsuit, if the property is protected by a homestead exemption. In the majority of cases, all liens based on money judgments are discharged.

The key exception to this rule is if the judicial lien arose out of a case in which you were found to be willful or malicious (such as injury or death caused by drunk driving). You also can't discharge any fines, penalties, or restitution that were imposed to punish you by a governmental agency.

Question 166: **How will my property be impacted differently if I file Chapter 13?**

The primary difference will be that you can keep your house even if you aren't current on your payments, because you will buy time using a repayment plan to get your mortgage up-to-date. When you develop a repayment plan, the first priority is to pay all your secured creditors. Whatever money is left over goes to your unsecured creditors. This allows you to focus on getting your mortgage current and keeping it there.

Question 167: **What is a cramdown?**

A cramdown is the ability to reduce a secured debt to the replacement value of the property. For example, if the value of your home has dropped below the amount of debt due on that loan, you can propose a plan in Chapter 13 bankruptcy that lets you pay off the replacement value of the home rather than the full outstanding mortgage amount. As long as you complete your Chapter 13 repayment plan, you will get to keep the property.

Question 168: **Can I continue my mortgage payments and keep my property if I file bankruptcy?**

Yes, you can continue to make your mortgage payments and keep your property in either Chapter 7 or Chapter 13 bankruptcy. But, if you have too much equity in your property and the amount of equity is above the homestead exemption, you will need to choose Chapter 13 bankruptcy to keep your property. If the bankruptcy trustee in a Chapter 7 bankruptcy determines there is enough value in the home to sell it, pay all sale costs, pay you the amount due based on your state's homestead exemption, and still have money left over to pay creditors, he or she will force the sale of your home. You can switch from a Chapter 7 to a Chapter 13 bankruptcy to avoid the sale of your home.

SEEKING HELP THROUGH CREDIT COUNSELING

You should seek the help of a credit counselor even before you get a Notice of Default on your property and long before your property faces foreclosure. The sooner you contact a credit counselor the better. In this chapter I review how credit counseling works and where to find a good counselor.

Question 169: **What is credit counseling?**

Credit counselors can advise you on how to manage your money better, provide solutions for your current financial problems, and help you develop a personalized plan that you can use to prevent future difficulties. They can offer you debt management plans, money management education, and homeowner counseling and education.

Many times credit counselors not only can help you come up with a plan for repaying your debt, but also work with your creditors to lower interest rates and develop a repayment plan so you will no longer receive harassing phone calls. Before losing your home or considering bankruptcy, you should first at least try credit counseling. If you do end up deciding you must file for bankruptcy, you will have taken a step that is required before you can file.

Question 170: What are the costs of credit counseling?

To keep your costs low, or possibly even free, you should work with a not-for-profit credit counseling agency. You can find those through the National Foundation for Credit Counseling (NFCC) at *www.debtadvice.org*. Some agencies offer free budget counseling and debt management services; others offer their services at fees or contributions that are affordable for consumers in debt. These are the fees that are suggested by the NFCC:

- Educational seminars are free and open to the public at most NFCC agencies.
- Most agencies can provide housing and mortgage counseling at no charge because they are funded by the U.S. Department of Housing.
- You can get one-on-one budget counseling for an average of $13.
- If you do enroll in a debt management plan, total average monthly fees are $14 plus an average startup fee of $23. Many times a debt management plan can even be offered free because the creditors contribute to the NFCC agencies.

If you are quoted higher fees, contact a different agency or the NFCC national office at (800) 388-2227.

Question 171: How do I find a reputable credit counselor?

Finding the right counselor is crucial to your success. Some agencies advertise that they are nonprofit, but are only concerned about their bottom line.

The first thing you should do when you start talking with a credit counselor is to find out if he or she belongs to a national organization, such as the NFCC, that requires members to adhere to a strict set of quality, financial, and ethical standards. Research the national organization and be certain you understand its practices.

Be sure that all payments you send as part of your debt management plan are sent to creditors in a timely manner. Some agencies may collect your first month's payment and call it a fee or donation and not send any money to your creditors. Ask the counselor how quickly the agency disburses your funds to creditors.

If a credit counselor promises to fix your credit report or score and settle your debt for very little money, be skeptical. If it sounds too good to be true, it probably is.

Make sure that your sessions with the counselor are substantive and that the counselor does truly take the time to understand your personal financial situation. For example, NFCC counselors usually spend about 90 minutes on the initial counseling appointment.

Be sure you are offered a range of services and not pushed into a profitable (for the agency) debt management plan. You should get a comprehensive budget review and a range of recommendations specific to your needs, not just get pushed into a plan.

Question 172: **What services should I seek to find?**

You should seek to find an agency that offers a range of services, including comprehensive budget planning, debt management plans, money management education, and homeowner counseling and education. If the only service an agency offers is a debt management plan, say no and find another agency.

Question 173: How are the employees of credit counseling firms paid?

You definitely want to ask that question during your initial interview. Some agencies are funded through contributions from creditors and consumers, but if contributions are suggested, be sure they are not higher than those discussed in Question 170.

Some agencies require that your first month's payment go into their pockets (and the pockets of their counselors) rather than sending the payment to your creditors. If that's the case, say no and move on to another, more reputable agency.

Question 174: What is a debt management plan?

A debt management plan is a systematic way to pay down your debt. A credit counseling agency will first do a comprehensive review of your current debt situation. Then the counselor will discuss numerous alternatives for getting you back on track, including budget management and money management education.

If your debt situation is very severe, the counselor may recommend a debt management plan as your best option for returning to financial health. You do need to have enough income to make the payments for a debt management plan to work. If your income is too low, the agency may recommend bankruptcy. At that point the agency will give you a certificate for the bankruptcy court (provided the counseling agency is approved by the court), so you can file your case.

Question 175: How does a debt management plan work?

If you enter into a debt management plan, you will be required to make monthly payments to the agency. The agency will then distribute these funds to your creditors.

By agreeing to participate in a debt management plan, your finance charges may be reduced or waived and your collection calls will be reduced. Some creditors may refuse to work with the credit counseling agency and will continue to call you.

When you have completed your debt management plan, the credit counseling agency will help you re-establish credit. It usually takes about 36 to 60 months to repay debts through a debt management plan. The time it will take depends on how much you owe and how much cash you have available to make the payments. An NFCC credit counseling agency will work with all your creditors, even if the creditors decide not to make a contribution to the agency.

Question 176: **What is a debt negotiation plan?**

Debt negotiation plans differ greatly from debt management plans. A debt negotiation specialist will collect money from you on a monthly basis while he or she negotiates for settlements with your creditors. Debt negotiation can be a very risky choice and can have a long-term negative impact on your credit report and your ability to get credit in the future. Many states have laws regulating debt negotiation companies and the services they offer. Before signing a contract with a debt negotiation company, be sure to contact your state attorney general for more information about laws in your state and to research the companies you are considering.

Question 177: **How does a debt negotiation plan work?**

If you hire a professional debt negotiator, he or she will try to reduce the principal on your debt as well as get any finance charges waived. During this period of negotiation, you will make monthly payments to the debt negotiator. These payments will be used to pay the negotiator's fees, as well as the lump sum needed to pay off your creditors.

In many cases a good debt negotiator can settle your debts at 30 to 70 percent less than your current principal. He or she will be able to negotiate different settlement agreements with each creditor. But beware—many people who promise debt reduction are not able to deliver and you end up wasting your money paying the negotiator monthly while your credit problems continue to grow. Also, be sure the debt negotiator gets agreements with your creditors to show the debt paid in full on your credit report, or your negative credit history will follow you for seven years after you settle.

In addition to checking out the debt negotiation firm with your state's attorney general, be certain to carefully read any contract you sign. A debt negotiation service can only help you if the debt has been turned over to a debt collection agency that is ready to make deals.

Question 178: **Are debt consolidation or debt reduction firms legitimate?**

Both types of firms can be legitimate, but there are many scam artists out there. In Questions 176 and 177 I discuss debt negotiation, which is what debt reduction firms specialize in. Debt consolidation can be offered by many different types of financial institutions. Even your own bank may offer debt consolidation loans.

However, you should be careful when considering debt consolidation. If you are consolidating your credit card debt to reduce your monthly payment and you will be converting unsecured debt (which can be discharged in a bankruptcy) with secured debt against your home, you may be putting your home at greater risk and just stalling the inevitable. You should only consider a consolidation loan if you truly plan to pay down that debt before starting to charge on your credit cards again.

The costs of consolidation loans can also add up. You may have to pay points, which is 1 percent of the amount you want to borrow, as well as other closing costs. These types of loans do offer a tax advantage because their interest is tax deductible, while the interest paid to credit card companies is not tax deductible.

Chapter 8

EXPLORING FORECLOSURE SALES

If the worst happens and you receive notice that your foreclosure sale has been scheduled, all is not lost. You may still be able to save your home. In this chapter I discuss the basics of how a foreclosure sale works and whether you can buy your home again even after a foreclosure sale.

Question 179: What is a public foreclosure auction?

If you don't find a way to reinstate your loan during the pre-foreclosure period, your home will be sold at a public foreclosure auction. Potential buyers will bid on your property in a competitive bidding process and the highest bidder, as long as he or she bids the minimum amount required by your lender, will win the auction.

Buyers often must pay cash at the auction and frequently don't have much time to research the title or the condition of the property. You will not have to deal with the buyer at all through this process.

In many states, after the sale is complete the new owner can send you a legal notice and ask you to vacate the premises in 72 hours. If you don't leave, the new owner can ask a judge to evict you. If you are willing to pay rent, you may be able to get a bit more time before you have to move. If you don't like the judge's decision, you do have a right to appeal it within 10 days, which can help you to buy more time.

Question 180: **What is an "as is" sale?**

All foreclosure sales are "as is" sales, which means the buyer must take the property in its current state and cannot ask you to do any repairs. In fact, a foreclosure property may not even be in insurable condition when the buyer completes the sale.

If some mistake was made by the lender or someone else during the foreclosure process, the sale could be ruled by a court to be flawed, which means the property could be tied up in legal proceedings for months or even years.

Question 181: **What is the right to redeem?**

In 25 states, the borrowers and any creditors with a stake in the property have the right to redeem the property, which means to buy it back after the foreclosure sale. The rules vary state by state: You can find out your state's rules on redemption at this Web site: *http://www.realtytrac.com/education/noframes/foreclosurePro.html*.

Question 182: **What is the process of appealing a foreclosure sale?**

If you find errors in your Notice of Default or in any other document relating to your foreclosure sale, you may be able to appeal the sale. Foreclosure documents can contain errors such as misspelled names, erroneous legal descriptions, inaccurate street addresses, and mathematical errors in calculating the amount due for legal fees, interest, and late payment charges. Any of the errors could make the process flawed and give you the right to appeal.

You also may notice that there were procedural errors during the service of documents or the lender failed to adhere to statutory foreclosure sale procedures, which could result in a court overturning a foreclosure sale. Sit down with an attorney and review not only the documents, but also the processes that were used. As you go through the foreclosure process, keep detailed notes about everything that happened. If there was a mistake, you will have the documentation needed to appeal a foreclosure and buy yourself time. The appeals process could take months.

Question 183: **What is equity skimming?**

Equity skimming is a scheme to take the equity from your property and leave you in even more of a financial mess. The most common type of equity skimmer is someone who offers to get you out of trouble by promising to pay your mortgage payments or promising you a large sum of cash when the property is sold. The equity skimmer suggests that you move out of your house immediately and give title to him or her, which means the equity skimmer would own the property, usually with an instrument called a "quitclaim deed." You may even be offered the possibility of staying in the property and paying rent.

The equity skimmer would then collect monthly rent, but not make any mortgage payments, allowing the lending institution to foreclose. You may believe that by signing over the property to the equity skimmer you can avoid foreclosure and any responsibility to the lender, but that's not true. If a "potential" buyer does not go through the full process of getting a loan and paying off yours, you are still responsible for the mortgage.

You can end up losing all your equity except for the small down payment the equity skimmer may have paid you to get you to sign the "quitclaim deed." Any rent the buyer collected before the lender forecloses is his to keep at the homeowner's expense. Keep your eyes open for equity skimmers.

The best way to avoid a problem is to ask an attorney or your mortgage company to review any deal you are offered. Attempt to get references and credit information from anyone offering to help bail you out. Check with the real estate commission or the district attorney's office to see if there are any complaints on file about the buyer. Don't sign any papers unless you are certain you understand what they are. Always get all promises in writing.

Question 184: **What is loan loss mitigation?**

Loss mitigation programs were created jointly by the federal government and the mortgage industry to come up with alternatives and help homeowners avoid foreclosures. Every homeowner's situation is unique, and each lender has its own way of developing programs that it can offer a borrower who is in trouble so he or she can avoid foreclosure.

There are a number of loss mitigation options, including mortgage modification (see Question 39), deed-in-lieu of foreclosure (see Question 185), short payoff or pre-foreclosure sale (see Question 186), repayment plan (see Question 88), special forbearance (see Question 38), or a partial claim (see Question 40).

All of these options are handled by your lender's loss mitigation department. If you are at least 90 days past due on your mortgage, work with the loss mitigation department to look at these options. You should also consider contacting a U.S. Department of Housing and Urban Development housing counseling agency to help you sort out your options. You can find one near you by using the search tool at HUD's Web site, *www.hud.gov*, or you can call HUD at (800) 569-4287.

Question 185: **What is a deed-in-lieu of foreclosure?**

If you have suffered a long-term financial hardship because of a job loss, loss of a key provider, or medical emergency, and you've tried to sell your home at fair market value for at least 90 days, you may be able to negotiate a deed-in-lieu of foreclosure through your lender's loss mitigation department. If successful, the lender will take possession of your property and you will owe nothing. Don't sign a deed-in-lieu of foreclosure if you could end up owing money on any deficiency between the sale price of the home (when the lender finally does sell it) and the amount still due on the loan. If the loan is more than the lender gets for the house, he or she could ask you to pay the deficiency and indicate on your credit report that you did not pay the loan in full. Be certain you can't face either of those possibilities before signing over your home voluntarily.

In order for the lender to consider a deed-in-lieu of foreclosure, you will need to complete a financial disclosure package and give the lender a copy of your active real estate listing agreement. The lender will only consider this option if there are no additional claims or liens against the property. That means you can't have a second mortgage, equity line, or any type of lien on record with the county. You will be giving up all rights to the property, and you will be turning over the property to the lender or other investor. It is possible that you will be asked to participate in a short payoff program, which is discussed in the next question.

Question 186: **What is a short payoff or pre-foreclosure sale?**

If you suffer a long-term financial hardship, during which time you are not able to maintain your mortgage loan, or if you must sell your property to avoid a loss of the property to foreclosure, you may be able to negotiate with the lender for a short payoff sale. In this case, the loss mitigation specialist may allow you to pay off less than the remaining amount due on the mortgage so you can sell the property. This is called a short payoff or pre-foreclosure sale. You must have identified a qualified buyer to use this option.

You should be aware that there could be tax ramifications with a short payoff or pre-foreclosure sale, so talk with your tax adviser before agreeing to this type of arrangement. In addition, some states do permit lenders to seek a deficiency judgment for the amount the payoff was discounted, so don't agree to any short sale without seeking the advice of an attorney.

Question 187: **When will lenders consider a short payoff sale?**

Short payoff sales are usually a lender's last resort before proceeding with a foreclosure. You are more likely to be successful with this strategy if the lender knows he will have a difficult time selling the property should he take possession after a foreclosure.

These situations are the most likely ones in which the lender will consider a short payoff sale:

- You bought the house, or refinanced it, at the top of a seller's market at an inflated price.
- You refinanced the property at 125 percent of its value, which was based on an overinflated property appraisal report.
- Property values have dropped significantly due to economic conditions.
- The property value of your home dropped below the amount of the loan balance.
- The property's "as is" condition is so bad the lender would not be able to sell it after a foreclosure.

Question 188: **What is a hardship test?**

All lenders have strict hardship tests that you must pass to get approval for a short payoff sale. The reasons one could be approved include these:

- The borrower or an immediate family member experienced a catastrophic illness that destroyed his or her financial position.
- The borrower's spouse died or the couple divorced and the borrower does not have sufficient income to make the mortgage payments.
- The borrower was transferred by his or her employer and can't sell the home.
- The borrower was called to active military duty for an extended period and can't make the mortgage payments.
- The borrower suffered a disabling illness or injury and can't work again.
- The borrower lost his or her job and has no chance to get a job given current economic conditions.
- The borrower is financially insolvent and there is no expectation for his or her financial situation to turn around in the near future.
- The borrower is in jail and doesn't have the income to make the mortgage payments.

Question 189: **What do lenders consider during the short payoff sale approval process?**

Lenders consider a number of factors when determining whether or not to agree to a short payoff sale, including:

- Your financial condition.
- Your property's "as is" value.

- The cost to put the property into resale condition.
- The property's value after repair.
- The cost of securing and maintaining the property while it is being marketed for sale.
- The cost of marketing and selling the property.

In addition to the factors involving you and the condition of the property, other factors that must be considered include the financial condition of the lender or the third-party investor on the mortgage, the loss mitigation policies of the lender and any investors, the procedures of a government agency that is insuring the loan (if applicable), and the number of underperforming loans the lender has.

Question 190: How does mortgage insurance impact foreclosure sales?

If you were required to buy mortgage insurance, which is the case if you put down less than 20 percent, the mortgage insurer would be obligated to pay any shortfall to the lender. If the lender declares your loan in default, the mortgage insurer may help you to keep your home by advancing you the funds needed to cure the default and reinstate the loan. In some cases the insurer may even purchase the loan from the lender and modify the repayment terms to match your income.

Question 191: What are the tax consequences of a short payoff sale?

The amount by which your lender reduces your debt in a short payoff sale is taxed as ordinary income unless the borrower is bankrupt or insolvent. Any time the amount canceled is more than $600, the lender must report the sale to the IRS on Form 1099C—Cancellation of Debt. You can find out more about how canceled debt is taxed in IRS publication 544, "Sales and Other Dispositions of Assets," at *http://www.irs.gov/publications /p544/index.html.*

Question 192: **What are compromise sales?**

If you are a veteran and you got your loan through the Department of Veterans Affairs (VA), you may be able to work out a compromise sale. This is the VA's version of a short payoff sale. A compromise sale is approved if, after reviewing the borrower's financial condition, the VA considers the loan in default to be impossible to fix. The borrower would have to be in a situation in which he or she cannot prevent the foreclosure of the property and cannot provide for his or her family.

Question 193: **What are the steps to complete a short payoff sale transaction?**

In most cases a short payoff transaction begins when you are contacted by a potential buyer who is interested in the property, but wants to pay less than needed to pay off the loan. You can contact the loss mitigation department and also give written authorization to the potential buyer so he or she can contact the loss mitigation department as well.

The loss mitigation department sends the borrower a short payoff sale package, which must be completed to start the approval process.

After completing the package and sending all required documents, the lender reviews the package and gets a property appraisal report to determine the as-is and as-repaired values. The lender then makes a decision on whether it will accept or reject the short payoff. If the lender rejects the short payoff amount, a counteroffer can be made. Once a payoff sale offer is accepted, the buyer closes on the short payoff transaction in 30 days.

Chapter 9

SPECIAL PROVISIONS FOR VICTIMS OF NATIONAL DISASTERS

I f you are a victim of a national disaster, you may be able to seek special help to avoid a foreclosure. In order to get this help, you must live in an area that was officially declared a national disaster by a presidential declaration. In this chapter, I discuss the special help you can get.

Question 194: What type of special assistance is available to a homeowner to avoid foreclosure, if I'm a victim of a national disaster?

In addition to aid from the Red Cross, the Salvation Army, and various governmental agencies, the Department of Housing and Urban Development offers special zero-down-payment mortgages with no up-front costs for disaster victims. These loans can help people whose homes have been severely damaged or destroyed. They can also help renters become homeowners.

If your home is still livable, but your finances were damaged so that you can't make your payments, the FHA, Fannie Mae, and

Freddie Mac (which back most of the mortgages on the market today) will declare a moratorium on foreclosures for at least 90 days. In some cases, such as Hurricane Katrina, the moratorium can be extended.

Question 195: Can I stop foreclosure if I'm eligible for grant assistance?

Yes, you can stop a foreclosure after a national disaster has been declared if you are eligible for grant assistance. After a major disaster, such as Hurricane Katrina, each state was allotted money from federal emergency funds to provide grants to home-owners so they could rebuild their homes.

Question 196: How do I apply for grant assistance?

If you were a victim of a national disaster, you should apply for assistance through the Federal Emergency Management Agency (FEMA). You can apply online at *www.fema.gov/assistance/index.shtm* or by calling (800) 621-3362.

Question 197: How can I work with my lender to delay foreclosure so I can buy time to apply for a grant or seek other assistance?

If your mortgage is near foreclosure, you will likely be in con-tact with your lender's loss mitigation department. Be certain to tell the specialist you are working with that you are a victim of a declared national disaster. Processes likely are in place to grant you a moratorium on the foreclosure. If the loss mitigation department is not helpful, contact a HUD housing counselor for assistance. You can find one near you by searching HUD's Web site at *www.hud.gov/offices*. You can also get help by calling HUD at (800) 569-4287.

Question 198: **Can HUD extend foreclosure deadlines for national disaster victims?**

Yes, HUD can and does extend foreclosure deadlines for national disaster victims. After a national disaster has been declared, HUD usually puts a 90-day moratorium in place for all FHA loans. Fannie Mae and Freddie Mac usually follow HUD's lead, and some private mortgage investors will as well. In a major disaster, this moratorium period can be extended.

Question 199: **If I'm in a federally declared disaster area, will my debt problems be reported to credit agencies?**

Many credit card companies, banks, credit unions, mortgage and finance companies, landlords, utility companies, and others do provide assistance to consumers trying to get their finances back in order after a national disaster, but you must call and ask for help.

Some will defer your payments or offer extended payment plans. Others will extend grace periods, waive late fees, or raise your credit limit. Many will refrain from reporting delinquencies and postpone collection, repossessions, and foreclosures.

If all else fails and you think you need additional assistance, contact the National Foundation for Credit Counseling (NFCC) and work with one of its credit counselors. You can call the foundation at (800) 388-2227. Many of the services provided by NFCC agencies are offered free or for very low cost.

Chapter 10

DISCOVERING STATE-BY-STATE FORECLOSURE AND HOMESTEAD EXEMPTION RULES

Each state enacts its own laws regarding how the foreclosure of a home should be carried out. If the state's laws are not followed exactly, you may have the right to appeal the foreclosure, so it's important to know the details of those laws.

In this chapter, I give you a brief overview of the laws so you can spot some obvious errors. Since your home is at stake, you should contact a real estate or bankruptcy attorney to learn more about your rights and what you must do to protect your home. You can find out more details about the foreclosure process on a state-by-state basis online at *http://www.drfg.com/info.php*.

If you are facing foreclosure, keep careful notes about everything that happens plus any paperwork you receive. If the foreclosure is successful, be sure your attorney reviews the details you've kept to see if there was an error committed upon which you can appeal.

The other way to stop a foreclosure at least temporarily is to file bankruptcy. A bankruptcy can't discharge a secured lien, such as a mortgage, but it may be able to buy you some time to bring your mortgage current and keep your home. In this chapter, I also discuss homestead exemptions, which give you some additional protection to help you save your home if you do file bankruptcy.

Question 200: **What are the foreclosure and homestead exemption rules specific to Alabama?**

Alabama lenders can foreclose on a property using either a judicial foreclosure or a non-judicial foreclosure. The non-judicial foreclosure is used when a power of sale clause exists in the deed of trust or mortgage.

In some deeds of trust, the power of sale clause will specify the time, place, and terms of a sale. If that is the case in your deed of trust, then that specified procedure must be followed. If not, the foreclosure sale takes place at the front or main door of the courthouse in the county where the property is located. The sale may take place 30 days after the last notice of sale is published, and the property will be sold for cash to the highest bidder. Notice of sale must be published once a week for four successive weeks in a newspaper published in the county or counties where the property is located. The notice of sale must give the time, place, and terms of sale along with a description of the property. If no power of sale is contained in a mortgage or deed of trust, the lender must file a lawsuit to foreclose after the mortgage or deed of trust is in default.

If your home is located in Alabama, you have a right of redemption for 12 months after the foreclosure sale. If you decide to file bankruptcy to stop the foreclosure, you can claim a homestead exemption of $5,000; the property in question cannot exceed 160 acres. You also must record a homestead declaration.

Question 201: What are the foreclosure and homestead exemption rules specific to Alaska?

Lenders in Alaska can foreclose on property using a judicial or non-judicial foreclosure. If a judicial foreclosure is used, the process is carried out according to the rules of equity; deficiency suits are permitted; and you will not have a right of redemption.

If a power of sale clause exists in your mortgage or deed of trust, the non-judicial foreclosure process will be used. If the power of sale clause specifies time, place, and terms of sale, that procedure is followed as long as it meets the minimum protections set forth in Alaska law. Here are the steps a lender must take to successfully complete a non-judicial foreclosure in Alaska:

1. Trustee must record a Notice of Default in the office of the recorder in the district where the property is located not less than 30 days after default and not less than three months before the sale.
2. The notice of default must include the name of the borrower, and the book and page where the deed is recorded. It also must describe the property and details about the borrower's default, the amount the borrower owes and the fact that the trustee wants to sell the property. Finally, it must include the date, time, and place of sale.
3. Within ten days of recording the notice of default, the trustee must send a copy by certified mail to the last known address of the borrower, the current occupant and any other individuals or companies that have a claim or lien on the property.
4. The borrower must be permitted to cure the default and stop the foreclosure by paying all past due amounts plus attorney's fees. The lender cannot require that the borrower repay the entire remaining principal balance to cure the default.

5. The sale of the property must take place at a public auction held at the front door of a courthouse of the superior court in the judicial district where the property is located. The trustee must sell the property to the highest bidder, which can be the lender.

If you decide to file bankruptcy to stop a foreclosure, you can claim a homestead exemption of $67,500. The Alaska exemption amounts can be adjusted by administrative order, so you should check those amounts if you are filing bankruptcy.

Question 202: What are the foreclosure and homestead exemption rules specific to Arizona?

Lenders in Arizona can use a judicial or non-judicial foreclosure process. The judicial foreclosure process is used when there is no power of sale clause in the mortgage or deed of trust.

For a non-judicial foreclosure, if the power of sale clause specifies the time, place, and terms of sale, those procedures are followed. If not, here are the procedures for carrying out a non-judicial foreclosure sale:

1. The trustee must record the notice of sale at the county recorder's office in the county in which the property is located. Within five days after recording the notice, the trustee must mail by certified mail a copy of the notice to any person named in the trust deed. He also must publish a notice in a newspaper in the county where the property is located once a week for four consecutive weeks. The last notice must be published not less than ten days prior to the sale.
2. The trustee or his agent must conduct the sale, which must be for cash to the highest bidder. If the lender is the highest bidder, he can make a "credit bid," which means he will cancel out all or part of the money the borrower owed the lender rather than pay cash.

3. The successful high bidder must pay the bid price by 5 P.M. the next business day after the bid. If the high bidder doesn't pay, the trustee may postpone the sale to another time and place.
4. After the sale is completed, the proceeds go to pay the obligations secured by the deed of trust that was foreclosed, and then the junior lien holders are paid. The successful bidder gets a trustee's deed.
5. If the amount paid at auction is less than the amount due, the lender cannot bring a deficiency suit against the person who lost the property if it is 2.5 acres or less and was a single-family or two-family dwelling. A deficiency suit is allowed on other types of property as long as it is filed within 90 days.

If you decide to file bankruptcy to stop the foreclosure, you can claim a homestead exemption up to $150,000. If you own more than one property, you should file a homestead declaration to clarify which property you want to claim as your homestead.

Question 203: **What are the foreclosure and homestead exemption rules specific to Arkansas?**

Arkansas lenders can foreclose on deeds of trust or mortgages using a judicial or non-judicial foreclosure process. Lenders must do an appraisal of the property before scheduling the date of foreclosure.

If a property is offered for sale and does not get an offer for two-thirds of the appraised value or more, the property must be offered for sale again in 12 months. At a second sale, the highest bidder gets the property without consideration of an appraisal.

If a judicial foreclosure is used, the court will decree the amount of the borrower's debt and give him or her a short time to pay that debt. If the borrower doesn't pay in that time, the clerk of the court advertises the property for sale. The lender may bid by crediting a portion (or all) of the amount the court found due to the lender against the sale price of the property. If the property does not sell for an amount equal to what is due, the lender may seize other property from the borrower. The borrower has one year from the date of sale to redeem the property by paying the amount at which the property was sold plus interest.

If a power of sale clause exists in the mortgage or deed of trust, a non-judicial foreclosure can be used. Here is the process for non-closure sales:

1. The trustee must record the notice of sale in the county recorder's office of the county where the property is located. The notice of default and intention to sell must be mailed by certified mail to the borrower within 30 days of the recording. Within five days after the notice is recorded the trustee must mail by certified mail a copy of the notice of sale to all parties to the trust deed. In addition the notice of default and intention to sell must appear in a county newspaper where the property is located once a week for four consecutive weeks with the last notice being published not less than 10 days prior to the date of sale. The notice must include the names of the parties to the mortgage or deed of trust, a legal description of the trust property and the street address of the property, the book and page numbers where the mortgage or deed of trust is recorded or the recorder's document number, the default involved, and the mortgagee's or trustee's intention to sell. Also a warning in large type must be included that states: "YOU MAY LOSE YOUR PROPERTY IF YOU DO NOT TAKE IMMEDIATE ACTION." The notice should also include the time, date, and place of sale.

2. Any person, including the lender, may bid at the sale. The high bidder must pay the bid at the time of the sale or within 10 days. The lender may bid by canceling out what is owed on the loan including unpaid taxes, insurance, costs of sale, and maintenance.

3. After the completion of the sale, the proceeds go toward paying the expenses of the foreclosure sale and then toward the obligations of the secured trust deed that was foreclosed. After that junior lien holders are paid. The original borrower is entitled to get any remaining funds. The successful bidder gets a trustee's deed.

The lender may sue the borrower for any deficiency of funds within 12 months of the power of sale foreclosure. The lender can sue for the difference between the foreclosure price and the balance due on the loan or the balance due on the loan minus the fair market value of the property, whichever is less.

If you decide to file for bankruptcy to stop foreclosure, you can claim a homestead exemption based on lot size. As long as your residence is on less than ¼ acre in a city, town, or village, or less than 80 acres elsewhere in the state, it is protected by the homestead exemption rules. If the property is between ¼ acre and 1 acre in a city, town, or village, or 80 to 160 acres elsewhere, an additional limit of $2,500 is provided. A homestead may not include property that is more than 1 acre in a city, town, or village, or 160 acres elsewhere.

Question 204: What are the foreclosure and homestead exemption rules specific to California?

California lenders can foreclose on deeds of trust or mortgages using either a judicial or non-judicial foreclosure process. If there is no power of sale clause, a judicial process is used. After the court orders a foreclosure, your home is auctioned to the highest bidder. Lenders can seek a deficiency judgment. Sometimes, the court will allow the borrower up to one year to redeem the property.

If there is a power of sale clause in the mortgage or deed of trust, the non-judicial foreclosure process is used. This includes:

1. The lender must record a notice of sale in the county where the property is located at least fourteen days prior to the sale and mail this notice by certified mail with return receipt requested, to the borrower at least 20 days before the sale. The lender must also post on the property itself at least 20 days before the sale, as well as post in at least one public place in the county where the property is to be sold. The notice of sale must contain the time and location of the sale; plus the property address; the trustee's name, address, and phone number; and a statement indicated that the property will be sold at auction.
2. The borrower can cure the default up to five days before the foreclosure sale to stop the process.
3. The sale can be held on any business day between the 9:00 A.M. and 5:00 P.M. It must take place at the location specified in the notice of sale. The property will be sold to the highest bidder and the trustee may require proof of the bidder's ability to pay their full bid amount.

Lenders may not seek a deficiency judgment after a non-judicial foreclosure sale, and the borrower has no rights of redemption.

California has two different homestead exemption systems that are used if you decide to file bankruptcy to save your home. One allows a homestead exemption of $50,000 if you are single and not disabled. Families are allowed a homestead exemption of $75,000 if no other member of the household has a homestead. People who are over age 65 or physically or mentally disabled can claim a homestead exemption of $150,000. You may file a homestead declaration to protect your property from the attachment of a judicial lien or protect the proceeds of a voluntary sale for six months. The second system allows up to an $18,675 homestead exemption on your residence.

Question 205: **What are the foreclosure and homestead exemption rules specific to Colorado?**

Colorado lenders can foreclose on mortgages or deeds of trust in default using either a judicial or non-judicial process. If a judicial process is used, the home will be auctioned off to the highest bidder if the court orders the foreclosure.

A non-judicial foreclosure is used if a power of sale clause exists in the mortgage or deed of trust. Here is the process for a power of sale foreclosure:

1. The lender, or more likely his or her attorney, begins the process by filing the required documents with the Office of the public trustee of the county where the property is located. The public trustee then files a "Notice of Election and Demand" with the county clerk and recorder of the county. After the notice is recorded, it must be published in a county newspaper where the property is located for a period of five consecutive weeks. In addition, the public trustee must mail the same information within ten days after the publication of the notice of election and demand for sale to the borrower and any owner or claimant of record at the address given in the recorded instrument. The public trustee must also mail within 21 days before the foreclosure sale a notice to the borrower that describes how to redeem the property.

2. The borrower may stop the foreclosure process by filing an "Intent to Cure" with the public trustee's office at least 15 days prior to the foreclosure sale. Then he or she must pay the necessary amount to bring the loan current by noon the day before the foreclosure sale is scheduled.

3. The foreclosure sale must be scheduled between 45 and 60 days after the recording of the election and demand for sale. The public trustee will likely hold the sale at any entrance to the courthouse, unless other provisions were made in the

deed of trust. Lenders do have the option to file a suit for deficiency in Colorado. Borrowers have up to 75 days after the sale to redeem the property by paying the foreclosure sale amount, plus interest.

If you choose to file for bankruptcy to stop a foreclosure, you can claim a homestead exemption of up to $45,000. A spouse or child of a deceased owner may claim the exemption.

Question 206: What are the foreclosure and homestead exemption rules specific to Connecticut?

Connecticut lenders must use a judicial foreclosure process to foreclose on a mortgage in default. The judicial foreclosure process is carried out by either a strict foreclosure or a decree of sale.

If a strict foreclosure is used, then no actual foreclosure sale is held. If the lender succeeds in getting a court order determining that the borrower is in default on his mortgage, the title transfers to the lender immediately. The court can establish a time in which the borrower may redeem the property. If the borrower fails to do so, the title goes to the lender and the borrower has no further claim to the property. The lender then has 30 days to record the certificate of foreclosure, which must contain a description of the property, the foreclosure proceedings, the mortgage, and the date the title transferred to the lender.

If the foreclosure is to be completed with a decree of sale, the court sets the time and manner of the sale and appoints a committee to sell the property. The court also appoints three appraisers to determine the value of the property. The borrower can stop the foreclosure any time before the sale by paying the balance due on the mortgage. Lenders may sue to obtain a deficiency judgment in Connecticut.

If you decide to file for bankruptcy to stop a foreclosure, you can claim a homestead exemption of up to $75,000.

Question 207: **What are the foreclosure and homestead exemption rules specific to Delaware?**

In Delaware, lenders must use a judicial foreclosure process to foreclose on a mortgage in default. Several different types of processes are possible, but the one used most often is called "scire facias." With this process the lender doesn't have to prove the borrower is in default on his mortgage; instead, the borrower must prove he isn't.

The suit to obtain a foreclosure order is filed by the lender. The borrower must appear to prove his case within 30 days of being served a writ, at which time he must provide evidence regarding why the foreclosure should not take place. If the court is not satisfied with the borrower's explanation and evidence, it will authorize a foreclosure sale.

The foreclosure sale must be conducted by the sheriff and held either at the courthouse or at the property itself at least 14 days after the notice of sale is posted on the property or other public places throughout the county in which the property is located. The buyer cannot redeem the property once the court has confirmed the sale.

Delaware offers no homestead exemption for those who file for bankruptcy. The only thing that can protect your property if you file for bankruptcy is the property being held in tenancy by the entirety, and only one spouse files for the bankruptcy.

Question 208: **What are the foreclosure and homestead exemption rules specific to Florida?**

Florida lenders must use a judicial foreclosure process to foreclose on a mortgage in default. If the foreclosure claim is tried, it will be done without a jury. Any court order will specify how the foreclosure must take place, and the foreclosure must be done on those terms.

Whatever the court orders—whether by legal advertisement, publication, or notice—it is the responsibility of the lender to be sure such actions are taken. After the sale takes place, the sales terms must be confirmed by the court that ordered the sale. The borrower has the right to redeem the property by paying the amount of the purchase price prior to the time of the sale confirmation by the court.

Until the sale is confirmed by the court, the buyer of the property will hold a certificate of sale. After the court confirms the sale, the buyers can file a certificate of title.

Lenders may sue to obtain a deficiency judgment in Florida.

If you choose to file for bankruptcy to stop a foreclosure, you can claim a homestead exemption of up to ½ acre in a municipality and 160 acres elsewhere in the state. A spouse or child of a deceased owner may claim the exemption. You may file a homestead declaration. Property held as tenancy by the entirety may be exempt against debts owed by only one spouse.

Question 209: **What are the foreclosure and homestead exemption rules specific to Georgia?**

Lenders in Georgia can foreclose on mortgages or deeds of trust using either a judicial or non-judicial foreclosure process. The judicial foreclosure process is used when no power of sale clause exists in the mortgage or deed of trust. Usually if the court orders a foreclosure, the property will be sold at auction to the highest bidder.

A non-judicial foreclosure is used when a power of sale clause exits. The process for a non-judicial foreclosure includes:

1. Notice must be mailed by certified mail, return receipt requested, to the borrower no later than 15 days prior to the date of the foreclosure sale to the address given to the lender by written notice from the borrower. The notice must be published in a county newspaper where the sale

will be held once a week for four weeks proceeding the sale.

2. All foreclosure sales are held the Tuesday of the month between 10:00 A.M. and 4:00 P.M. at the courthouse.

Lenders can seek a deficiency judgment in Georgia.

If you decide to file bankruptcy to stop the foreclosure, you can claim a homestead exemption of up to $10,000.

Question 210: **What are the foreclosure and homestead exemption rules specific to Hawaii?**

Lenders in Hawaii can use either a judicial or non-judicial foreclosure process. The judicial process involves a lawsuit to obtain a court order to foreclose if there is no power of sale clause in the mortgage or deed of trust. If the court orders a foreclosure, the property will likely be sold at auction to the highest bidder.

If a power of sale clause does exist, then a non-judicial foreclosure will be used.

Here is the process for the non-judicial foreclosure process:

1. The lender files a notice of intent to foreclose, which must be published in a newspaper with general circulation in the county where the property is located once a week for three successive weeks. In addition, copies of the notice must be mailed or delivered to the mortgagor, the borrower, any prior or junior creditors and the state director of taxation. Also, the notice must be posted on the premises not less than 21 days before the day of sale. Notice must include the date, time, and place of the public sale; the dates and times of the two open houses of the property or a statement that there will be no open houses; the money owed to the mortgagee under the mortgage agreement; description of the mortgaged property, including the address or description of the location and the tax map key number of

the property; the name of the mortgagor and the borrower; the name of the lender; the name of any prior or junior creditors that had a recorded lien on the property before a notice of default was recorded; the name, the address, and the telephone number of the person conducting the public sale; and the terms and conditions of the public sale.

2. The borrower may cure the default up to three days before the sale and stop the foreclosure by paying the lien debt, as well as any costs and reasonable attorney's fees, unless another agreement is made between the lender and the borrower.

3. The sale can be held no earlier than 14 days after the last ad is published. The property will be sold at auction to the highest bidder.

Hawaii offers no rights of redemption to the borrower.

If you decide to file bankruptcy to stop a foreclosure, you can claim a homestead exemption. Hawaii offers a head of family over age 65 a $30,000 homestead exemption. All others can get up to a $20,000 homestead exemption. Property held as tenancy by the entirety may be exempt against debts owed by only one spouse.

Question 211: **What are the foreclosure and homestead exemption rules specific to Idaho?**

Idaho lenders can foreclose on deeds of trust in default using a non-judicial foreclosure process. Here is how the process works in Idaho:

1. A notice of sale must be recorded in the county where the property is located and given to the borrower and the occupants of the property (if not the borrower) at least 120 days before the date of the sale. In addition the notice must be published in the county newspapers where the property is located at least once a week for four consecutive weeks. The

final ad must be run at least 30 days before the foreclosure. The published notice must include a legal description of the property, its street address, and the name and phone number of someone who can give directions to the property. The notice also must include the nature of the default; a legal description of the property; as well as its street address; the lender's name; the date, time, and place of the sale; and the name and phone number of the person conducting the sale.

2. The foreclosure sale must take place at the date, time, and place specified in the notice, but the sale may be postponed and held at a new time and place within 30 days of the originally scheduled sale.

   The borrower can redeem the property during a six month period if the property is less than 20 acres. If the property is more than 20 acres, the borrower has one year to redeem the property.

If you decide to file bankruptcy to stop the foreclosure, you can claim a homestead exemption up to $50,000. You must record a homestead exemption for property that is not yet occupied.

Question 212: **What are the foreclosure and homestead exemption rules specific to Illinois?**

Lenders in Illinois have three different options to foreclose on a mortgage in default—a judicial foreclosure, a deed-in-lieu of foreclosure, and a consent foreclosure. Here are how the three options work:

If a judicial foreclosure is used then the lender must give the borrower a notice of intent to foreclose at least 30 days prior to the court's foreclosure judgment. If the court finds in favor of the lender and issues a notice of sale, the sale must be conducted based on the terms and conditions specified by the court.

The sheriff or any judge within the county where the property is located may conduct the sale. The borrower has no rights of redemption after the foreclosure sale.

If the borrower and lender reach agreement for a deed-in-lieu of foreclosure, the borrower may give the deed to the lender and his interests in the property are terminated. If the lender agrees and accepts the deed, it can't seek to obtain a deficiency judgment against the borrower.

If the court orders a consent foreclosure to satisfy the mortgage by giving title to the property to the lender then the borrower has no right of redemption. The lender also may not file for a deficiency judgment.

If you decide to file bankruptcy to stop foreclosure, you can claim a $7,500 homestead exemption. A spouse or child can claim the homestead exemption of a deceased owner. Illinois does recognize tenancy by the entirety with some limitations.

Question 213: **What are the foreclosure and homestead exemption rules specific to Indiana?**

Indiana lenders must use the judicial foreclosure process to close on a mortgage in default. Usually after the court orders a foreclosure, the property will be auctioned to the highest bidder.

In Indiana, there is a waiting time between the date the suit is filed and the day the property is sold. The date the mortgage was signed determines the length of time a lender must wait between filing the suit and proceeding with the foreclosure sale; this can vary from 3 to 12 months. The owner may file a waiver of the time limit, which allows the sale to proceed without delay. If the borrower waives the wait time, the lender can file for a deficiency judgment.

If a foreclosure sale is ordered by the court, the lender must publish an ad once a week for three weeks. The first ad must be run 30 days before the sale. At the time the first ad is run, each owner must be served with notice of the foreclosure sale by the sheriff. The sheriff conveys title by a deed given immediately after the sale. The owner may reside in the property, rent free, until the foreclosure sale, provided the owner is not destroying the property.

If you choose to file bankruptcy to stop a foreclosure, you can claim a homestead exemption of $7,500.

Question 214: **What are the foreclosure and homestead exemption rules specific to Iowa?**

Iowa lenders can foreclose on a mortgage in default using either a judicial or alternative non-judicial foreclosure process. For a judicial foreclosure the lender must file a suit against the borrower and obtain a decree of sale from the court that has jurisdiction in the county where the property is located. If the court finds the borrower in default, it will give a set period to pay the delinquent amount plus costs. If the borrower doesn't pay within that period of time, the court will order that the property be sold.

A notice of the sale must be posted in at least three public places in the county. One must be at the county courthouse. In addition, the lender should publish the notice in two weekly publications printed in the county. The first publication must be at least four weeks before the date of sale and the second at a later time before the sale. If the borrower occupies and possesses the property, he or she must be served the notice at least 20 days prior to the sale. The sale must be at public auction, between 9:00 A.M. and 4:00 P.M. The date must be stated clearly in the notice of sale. The highest bid wins the auction.

Iowa borrowers can avoid a foreclosure suit by voluntarily conveying all of their rights in the property secured by the mortgage to the lender. If the lender accepts the conveyance from the borrower, the lender is given immediate access to the property. The lender must waive any rights to file for a deficiency judgment against the borrower if the property is voluntarily conveyed. In addition, the borrower must sign a "disclosure of notice and cancellation," to indicate that he or she is voluntarily giving up the right to reclaim or occupy the property. The borrower and lender must file a joint document with the county recorder's office indicating they have chosen to proceed with the foreclosure using the voluntary foreclosure procedures.

If you choose to file bankruptcy to stop a foreclosure, you can claim a homestead exemption at an unlimited property value, provided the property does not exceed ½ acre in a town or city or 40 acres elsewhere. You should record a homestead declaration.

Question 215: **What are the foreclosure and homestead exemption rules specific to Kansas?**

Kansas lenders can foreclose on a mortgage in default using the judicial foreclosure process. Usually, after the court orders a fore-closure, the property will be auctioned to the highest bidder.

If a property is to be sold at a foreclosure auction, the notice of the time of sale must be advertised once a week for three consecutive weeks, with the last publication being no more than 14 days and no less than 7 days before the sale. The borrower must receive a notice of the sale within five days of the first advertisement.

Unless the court specifies otherwise, the sale is held at the courthouse of the county in which the property is located. The highest bidder wins the sale and will receive a certificate of pur-chase. After the sale is confirmed, the winning bidder gets a sheriff's deed. The borrower has a right of redemption for 12 months from the date of the foreclosure sale. Lenders may sue for a deficiency judgment.

If you decide to file for bankruptcy to stop a foreclosure, you can claim a homestead exemption of unlimited value as long as the property is less than 1 acre in a town or city or 160 acres on a farm.

Question 216: What are the foreclosure and homestead exemption rules specific to Kentucky?

Kentucky lenders can foreclose on a mortgage in default by using the judicial foreclosure process. Usually the court decrees the amount of the borrower's debt and gives him or her a short time to pay. If the borrower doesn't pay within that time, the clerk of the court advertises the property for sale.

Property must be appraised prior to the scheduled date of foreclosure. If the foreclosure sale price is less than two-thirds of the appraised value, the borrower has one year from the date of the sale to redeem the property. To do so, he or she must pay the amount for which the property was sold plus interest.

Lenders can obtain a deficiency judgment against the borrower for the difference between the amount the borrower owed on the original loan and the foreclosure sale price, but only if the borrower was personally served with the lawsuit or failed to answer.

If you choose to file a bankruptcy to stop a foreclosure, you can claim a homestead exemption of $5,000.

Question 217: What are the foreclosure and homestead exemption rules specific to Louisiana?

Louisiana lenders may foreclose on a mortgage in default by using one of two judicial foreclosure processes—executory and ordinary. The ordinary process involves filing a suit and getting a court order, after which the property is sold.

The executory process takes place when the lender uses a mortgage that includes an "authentic act that imparts a confession of judgment," which is a statute unique to Louisiana. If this statute is used, it means the borrower signed and acknowledged the obligations of the mortgage in the presence of a notary public and two witnesses. This type of mortgage makes the foreclosure process easier for the lender because once the suit is filed and the original note and a certified copy of the mortgage are provided, the court will issue an order for the process to begin.

Once the court orders an executory process, the borrower must be served with a demand for the delinquent payments. The borrower has three days to pay or the court will order a writ of seizure. The sale of the property will be held after being advertised for 30 days.

Lenders may also sue to obtain a deficiency judgment. Buyers have no rights of redemption.

If you choose to file a bankruptcy to stop a foreclosure, you can claim a $25,000 homestead exemption. If the debt is the result of catastrophic or terminal illness or injury one year before filing a bankruptcy, the value of the homestead exemption is unlimited provided the property is less than 5 acres in a city or town or 200 acres elsewhere in the state.

Question 218: **What are the foreclosure and homestead exemption rules specific to Maine?**

Maine lenders may foreclose on mortgages in default using either a judicial or strict foreclosure process. Although Maine does allow lenders to pursue foreclosure by judicial methods, which involves filing a lawsuit to obtain a court order to foreclose, it is only used in special circumstances. The primary method of foreclosure in Maine is strict foreclosure.

The strict foreclosure process is based on Maine's foreclosure doctrine, which states that the lender owns the property until the mortgage is paid in full. If the borrower breaks any conditions of the mortgage before being paid in full, the borrower loses any right to the property. The lender can take possession of the property or arrange for its sale.

The borrower has a redemption period of three months (pre-1975 mortgages) or 12 months (post-1975 mortgages). If the lender takes possession of the property, it must hold possession of it for the entire redemption period to finalize the foreclosure.

If the lender chooses to sell the property without taking possession of it first, it must file an initial suit and then wait until the end of the redemption period to sell the property according to special procedures set by the court. Lenders may file for a deficiency judgment, but it is limited to the difference between the fair market value, as determined by an appraisal, and the balance of the loan in default.

If you choose to file for bankruptcy to stop a foreclosure, you can claim a homestead exemption up to $35,000. If the debtor has minor dependents or is over the age of 60 or physically or mentally disabled, the homestead exemption is $70,000.

Question 219: **What are the foreclosure and homestead exemption rules specific to Maryland?**

Maryland lenders that want to foreclose on a mortgage or deed of trust in default can use one of three methods: judicial foreclosure, an assent to decree, or non-judicial foreclosure. If the security instrument does not contain a power of sale clause or an assent to a decree clause, the lender must file a suit against the borrower and obtain a decree of sale from a court that has jurisdiction in the county where the property is located before foreclosure proceedings can begin. The court determines whether a default has occurred.

If the court finds that a default has occurred, it sets the amount of the debt, interest, and costs then due, and provides a reasonable time within which payment must be made if the borrower wants to keep the property. The court may order that if payment is not made within the time fixed in the order, the property must be sold to satisfy the debt.

If an assent to a decree foreclosure exists in the security document, the lender must file a complaint to foreclose on the property. It is easier than an ordinary foreclosure, because a hearing does not need to be held prior to the foreclosure sale.

If a power of sale clause exists in the mortgage or deed of trust, a non-judicial foreclosure process can be used. Lenders must still file with the court before the foreclosure process can begin, but a hearing is not necessary. Once foreclosure begins the process includes:

- A notice of sale is published in a county newspaper where the property is located at least once a week for three successive weeks. The first publication cannot be less than 15 days prior to sale. The last publication cannot be more than one week prior to sale. The notice of sale must also be sent to the borrower at his or her last known address by certified and registered mail not more than 30 days and not less than 10 days before the sale.
- The sale must be conducted by a person authorized to make the sale, such as the trustee or sheriff, and may take place immediately outside the courthouse entrance, on the property itself, or at the location advertised in the notice of sale.
- Within 30 days after the sale, the person authorized to make the sale must file a complete report of the sale with the court. The clerk of the court then issues a notice with a brief description identifying the property and stating the sale will be ratified unless appealed within 30 days after the date of the notice. A copy of the notice will be published at least once a week in each of three successive weeks before the expiration of the 30-day period in one or more county newspapers.

  Lenders have three years to file for a deficiency judgment, which is limited to the balance of the loan in default after the foreclosure sale proceeds have been applied.

Maryland has no homestead exemption. If you hold title as tenancy by the entirety, the property will be exempt from bankruptcy if the debts involved are owed by only one spouse.

Question 220: **What are the foreclosure and homestead exemption rules specific to Massachusetts?**

Massachusetts lenders may foreclose on deeds of trust or mortgages in default using either a foreclosure by possession or non-judicial foreclosure process. If a lender chooses to use the foreclosure by possession process after the borrower defaults on the mortgage, the lender can take possession of the property by obtaining a court order, entering the property peaceably, and getting consent of the buyer. After the lender maintains possession peaceably for three years, the borrower loses all rights of redemption.

If a power of sale clause exists in a mortgage or deed of trust, a non-judicial foreclosure process can be used. This process includes:

- Recording a notice of sale in the county where the property is located. The notice also must be sent, by registered mail, to the borrower at his or her last known address at least 14 days prior to the foreclosure sale. In addition it must be published once a week for three weeks, with the first publication at least 21 days before the sale, in a county newspaper of general circulation in the county where the property is located. The notice must include the place, time, and date of the foreclosure hearing; the date the mortgage was recorded; the borrower's name; the amount of the default and the terms of the sale.
- The sale must be by public auction on the date, time, and place specified in the notice of sale and the property sold to the highest bidder.

If you want to file bankruptcy to stop the foreclosure of the property, you can claim a $500,000 bankruptcy exemption. You must record a homestead declaration if it is not in the title to the property before filing for bankruptcy.

Question 221: **What are the foreclosure and homestead exemption rules specific to Michigan?**

Michigan lenders may foreclose on deeds of trust or mortgages in default using either a judicial or non-judicial foreclosure process. In judicial foreclosure, a court decrees the amount of the borrower's debt and gives him or her a short time to pay. If the borrower fails to pay within that time, the court will issue a notice of sale.

If a power of sale clause exists in the deed of trust, a non-judicial foreclosure can be used. Here is the non-judicial foreclosure process:

- A notice of sale must be published once a week for four weeks in a newspaper with general circulation in the county where the property is located. The notice must also be posted on the property at least 15 days after the first notice of sale is published. The notice must contain the borrower's and lender's name; a description of the property; the terms of the sale; and the time, place, and date of the sale.
- The trustee or the sheriff of the county may conduct the sale between the hours of 9:00 A.M. and 4:00 P.M. on the date specified in the notice of sale.
- The sale must be made at public auction and sold to the highest bidder.

If you want to file bankruptcy to stop the foreclosure of the property, you can claim a homestead exemption of $3,500 provided the property is on one lot in a town, village, or city, or 40 acres elsewhere. A spouse or child of a deceased owner may claim the homestead exemption. If the property is held as tenancy by the entirety, it may be exempt from debts owed by just one spouse.

Question 222: **What are the foreclosure and homestead exemption rules specific to Minnesota?**

Minnesota lenders may foreclose on deeds of trust or mortgages in default using either a judicial or non-judicial foreclosure process. The judicial process involves filing a lawsuit to obtain a court order to foreclose and must be used when no power of sale clause is present in the mortgage or deed of trust. Usually after the court declares a foreclosure, the home will be auctioned to the highest bidder.

If there is a power of sale clause in the mortgage or deed of trust, a non-judicial foreclosure will be used. The process for a non-judicial foreclosure includes:

1. A notice of sale must contain the borrower and lender names; the original loan amount and current amount of default; the date of the mortgage; a description of the property; and the time, place and date of the foreclosure sale and must be recorded in the county where the property is located.

2. The sheriff of the county in which the property is located conducts the sale on the date specified in the notice of sale. The property is sold to the highest bidder, who will receive certificate of sale.

   Lenders may pursue a deficiency judgment, but it is limited to the difference between the fair market value of the property and the unpaid balance of the original loan. Borrowers have up to one year to redeem the property by paying the past due amount on the loan.

If you want to file for bankruptcy to stop a foreclosure, you can claim a homestead exemption of $200,000. If the homestead is used for agricultural purposes, a $500,000 exemption is provided. The property cannot exceed ½ acre in the city or 160 acres elsewhere.

Question 223: What are the foreclosure and homestead exemption rules specific to Mississippi?

Mississippi lenders may foreclose on deeds of trust or mortgages in default using either a judicial or non-judicial foreclosure process. The judicial process is used when no power of sale clause is present in the mortgage or deed of trust. Usually after the court declares a foreclosure, the home will be auctioned to the highest bidder.

If a power of sale clause exists in a mortgage or deed of trust, a non-judicial foreclosure is used. The non-judicial foreclosure process includes:

1. The trustee records a notice of sale that includes the borrower's name and the date, time, and place of the sale in the county where the property is located. This notice must be posted at the courthouse door in the county where the property is located and published in a newspaper of general circulation in the county for a period of three consecutive weeks before the sale.
2. The borrower may cure the default and stop the foreclosure before the foreclosure sale by paying the delinquent payments plus costs and fees
3. The sale may be held in the county where the property is located or in the county where the borrower resides. In either case, the sale must be conducted at the normal location for sheriff's sales within the given county. Borrowers who lose their property as the result of a non-judicial foreclosure have no rights of redemption in Mississippi.
4. The property must be made at public auction for cash to the highest bidder.

If you choose to file bankruptcy to stop the foreclosure process, you can claim a homestead exemption of $75,000. The property cannot exceed 160 acres. A mobile home does not qualify for a homestead exemption unless you own the land on which it is located.

Question 224: **What are the foreclosure and homestead exemption rules specific to Missouri?**

Missouri lenders may foreclose on a deed of trust or mortgages in default using either a judicial or non-judicial foreclosure process. The judicial foreclosure process is used when no power of sale clause is present in the mortgage or deed of trust. Usually after the court declares a foreclosure, the home will be auctioned to the highest bidder.

If a power of sale clause is present in the mortgage or deed of trust, a non-judicial foreclosure process can be used. Here is the way that process works:

1. A notice of sale must be mailed to the borrower at his or her last known address at least 20 days prior to the scheduled day of sale. The notice of sale must also be published in a newspaper within the county.
2. The sale is conducted by the trustee at public auction and sold to the highest bidder for cash. The lender may bid on the property. If the lender is the winning bidder, the borrower has 12 months to redeem the property.

If you choose to file for bankruptcy to stop the foreclosure, you can claim a homestead exemption up to $15,000. If you own a mobile home, the exemption is only up to $5,000. Property held as tenancy by the entirety may be exempt against debts if they are owed by only one spouse.

Question 225: **What are the foreclosure and homestead exemption rules specific to Montana?**

Montana lenders may foreclose on deeds of trust or mortgages in default using either a judicial or non-judicial foreclosure process. When a judicial foreclosure is used, the court decrees the amount of the borrower's debt and gives him or her a short time to pay. If the borrower does not pay the debt within the time given, the court will issue a notice of sale. If a power of sale clause exists in a mortgage or deed of trust, the non-judicial foreclosure process is used. This process includes:

1. A notice of sale must be recorded in the county where the property is located. The notice is then mailed, by registered or certified mail, to the borrower at his or her last known address at least 120 days before the foreclosure sale. In addition it is published once a week for three successive weeks in a newspaper of general circulation in the county where the property is located and posted on the property at least 20 days before the foreclosure sale. The notice must include the time, date, and place of sale; the borrower's, lender's and trustee's names; a description of both the property and the amount in default; and the book and page where the deed is recorded.
2. The trustee must conduct the foreclosure sale between the hours of 9:00 A.M. and 4:00 P.M. at the courthouse in the county where the property is located. The property must be sold at public auction to the highest bidder.

   Lenders may not obtain a deficiency judgment against the borrower and the borrower has no rights of redemption.

If you choose to file bankruptcy to stop the foreclosure, you can claim a $100,000 homestead exemption. You must record a homestead declaration before filing the bankruptcy.

Question 226: What are the foreclosure and homestead exemption rules specific to Nebraska?

Nebraska lenders may foreclose on a mortgage in default using the judicial foreclosure process. The court decrees the amount of the borrower's debt and then gives him or her a short time to pay. If the borrower fails to pay within that time, the clerk of the court advertises the property for sale.

The court may order the entire property to be sold, or just a part of it. The sale can be delayed for up to nine months after the court's decree if the borrower files a written request for a delay with the clerk of the court within 20 days after the judge's order. If the borrower doesn't ask for the delay, the process of the sale of the property can start 20 days after the judgment. The borrower has the right to cure the default at any time while the suit is pending by paying the delinquent amount owed plus any interest and costs that have built up.

The sheriff must give public notice of the time and place of the sale by posting the notice on the courthouse door; posting the notice in at least five other public places in the county where the property is located; and by advertising the property for sale once a week for a period of four weeks in a newspaper published in the county. The court must confirm the sale after it takes place. Once the sale is confirmed, the borrower has no right of redemption.

If you decide to file bankruptcy to stop the foreclosure process, you can claim up to $12,500 as a homestead exemption, but the property cannot exceed two lots in a village or city or 160 acres elsewhere.

Question 227: What are the foreclosure and homestead exemption rules specific to Nevada?

Nevada lenders may foreclose on deeds of trust or mortgages in default using either a judicial or non-judicial foreclosure process.

The judicial process of foreclosure is used when no power of sale clause exists in the mortgage or deed of trust. Usually after the court declares a foreclosure, the home will be auctioned to the highest bidder. The borrower can redeem the property for up to 12 months after the sale if the judicial foreclosure process is used.

If there is a power of sale clause in the mortgage or deed of trust, a non-judicial foreclosure is used. The process for this type of foreclosure is:

1. A notice of default and election to sell must be mailed certified, return receipt requested, to the borrower at his or her last known address on the date the notice is recorded in the county where the property is located. Beginning on the day after the notice of default and election was recorded with the county and mailed to the borrower, the borrower has between 15 to 35 days to cure the default by paying the delinquent amount on the loan. The actual amount of time allowed depends on the date of the original deed of trust.
2. An owner can stop the foreclosure process by filing an "Intent to Cure" with the Public Trustee's office at least 15 days prior to the foreclosure sale. He or she then must pay the money needed to bring the loan current by noon the day before the foreclosure sale is scheduled.
3. The foreclosure sale will be held at the place, time, and date stated in the notice of default and election.

   Lenders have three months after the sale to try and obtain a deficiency judgment. Borrowers have no rights of redemption.

If you decide to file bankruptcy to stop the foreclosure, you can claim up to $200,000 as a homestead exemption. You must record your homestead declaration before filing for bankruptcy.

Question 228: **What are the foreclosure and homestead exemption rules specific to New Hampshire?**

New Hampshire has five methods of foreclosure that can be used. These include a judicial foreclosure, a non-judicial foreclosure process, and three special methods: Entry under Process, Entry and Publication, and Possession and Publication.

The judicial foreclosure process is a strict foreclosure process wherein the lender files a complaint against the borrower and obtains a decree of sale from a court that has jurisdiction in the county where the property is located in order to start the foreclosure process. Usually if the court finds the borrower in default, it will give the borrower a set period of time to pay the delinquent amount plus costs. If the borrower does not pay within that period of time, the court will order the property be sold. Anyone can bid at the foreclosure sale, including the lender.

If the mortgage or deed of trust has a power of sale clause, a non-judicial foreclosure is used. Here is how that type of foreclosure works:

1. The lender records a notice of sale in the county where the property is located and mails the notice to the borrower at least 25 days before the sale. In addition the lender publishes the notice once a week for three weeks, with the first publication appearing more than 20 days before the sale in a newspaper with general circulation in the county where the property is located.
2. The notice must include the time, date, and place of sale; a description of the property and the default; as well as a "warning" to the borrower. The warning must inform him or her that the property is going to be sold and explain any rights he or she may have to stop the foreclosure.
3. The foreclosure sale must be held on the property itself, unless the power of sale clause specifies a different location.

New Hampshire's special foreclosure methods are:

- **Entry under Process:** With this method, the lender enters the property under process of law and maintains actual possession of the property for one year to complete the foreclosure.
- **Entry and Publication:** With this method, the lender enters the property peaceably and takes continued actual, peaceable possession for a period of one year. In addition, the lender publishes a notice in a newspaper of general circulation in the county where the property is located, stating the time of possession, the lender's and borrower's names, the date of the mortgage, and a description of the property. The notice must be published for three successive weeks, with the first publication appearing at least six months before the borrower's right to redeem has expired.
- **Possession and Publication:** With this method, the lender who has possession of the property publishes a notice stating that from and after a certain day, the property will be held for default of the mortgage and the borrower's rights to the property will be foreclosed. This notice must be published for three successive weeks in a newspaper printed in the county where the property is located and must give the borrower's and lender's names, the date of the mortgage, a description of the property, and the lender's intention to hold possession of the property for at least one year.

Borrowers have no rights of redemption when any of these three special methods of foreclosure are used.

If you decide to file bankruptcy to stop one of these foreclosure processes, you can claim a homestead exemption up to $100,000.

Question 229: **What are the foreclosure and homestead exemption rules specific to New Jersey?**

New Jersey lenders may foreclose on a mortgage in default by using the judicial foreclosure process. After the court decrees the amount of the borrower's debt, it gives the borrower a short time to pay. If the borrower fails to pay the debt within that time, the clerk of the court advertises the property for sale.

Once the foreclosure process begins, a foreclosure notice must be posted in the county office in the county in which the property is located; posted on the property in foreclosure; and published in two newspapers in the county. The lender must also notify the borrower at least ten days prior to the foreclosure sale.

Lenders can obtain a deficiency judgment. Borrowers have a right to redemption and/or objection within ten days after the sale.

New Jersey offers no homestead exemption in bankruptcy, but if the title of the property is held as tenancy by the entirety and the debt is owed by only one spouse, bankruptcy by the spouse in debt could stop the foreclosure, because the spouse not in debt does have an exemption.

Question 230: **What are the foreclosure and homestead exemption rules specific to New Mexico?**

New Mexico lenders may foreclose on a mortgage in default by using the judicial foreclosure process. A court will decree the amount of the borrower's debt and give him or her a short time to pay. If the borrower doesn't pay within that time, the court issues a notice of sale. The notice of sale must contain a legal description of the property, as well as state the place, time, and date of the sale. The sale must be at least 30 days after the notice of sale is issued. The property will then be sold to the highest bidder on the date specified in the notice.

In most cases, the borrower has up to nine months to redeem the property by paying the amount of the highest bid at the foreclosure sale plus costs and interest.

A non-judicial foreclosure is only available for commercial and business properties valued at over $500,000.

If you do decide to file bankruptcy to stop the foreclosure, you can claim a homestead exemption up to $30,000.

Question 231: What are the foreclosure and homestead exemption rules specific to New York?

New York lenders may foreclose on deeds of trust or mortgages in default using either a judicial or non-judicial foreclosure process. Using the judicial foreclosure process, the lender files a complaint against the borrower and obtains a decree of sale from a court having jurisdiction in the county where the property is located. Once the court issues that decree, foreclosure proceedings can begin. Usually the court will give the borrower a set period of time to pay the delinquent amount plus costs. If the borrower doesn't pay within the time allotted, the court will order the property sold by the sheriff of the county or a referee. In most situations, the foreclosure sale is advertised for four to six weeks. The property is then sold by public auction to the highest bidder. Anyone may bid, including the lender.

After the property is sold, the officer conducting the sale must execute a deed to the purchaser. The officer must also pay the debt owed using the proceeds of the sale and then obtain a receipt for payment from the lender. Within 30 days after completing the sale, the officer must file with the clerk of the court a report of sale, which must include the receipt from the lender. Unless otherwise ordered by the court, the sale can't be confirmed until three months after the filing of the report of sale.

If the mortgage or deed of trust includes a power of sale clause, a non-judicial foreclosure is used. Even though this type of foreclosure is allowed in New York, it is rarely used by lenders.

If you decide to file bankruptcy to stop the foreclosure, you can claim a $10,000 homestead exemption.

Question 232: What are the foreclosure and homestead exemption rules specific to North Carolina?

North Carolina lenders may foreclose on deeds of trust or mortgages in default using either a judicial or non-judicial foreclosure process. The judicial process involves filing a lawsuit to obtain a court order to foreclose. Usually after the court declares a foreclosure, the home is auctioned to the highest bidder.

If the mortgage or deed of trust includes a power of sale clause, a non-judicial foreclosure is used. In North Carolina, a preliminary hearing must be held before a power of sale foreclosure can take place. Here is the process for a non-judicial foreclosure:

1. The lender must send a notice of sale by first-class mail to the borrower at least 20 days before the sale. He or she also must publish the notice in a newspaper of general circulation in the county where the property is located once a week for two successive weeks, with the last ad being published not less than ten days before the sale. In addition the notice must be posted on the courthouse door for 20 days prior to the foreclosure sale. The notice must include the names of borrowers and lenders, as well as provide a description of the property. It also must state the date, time, and place of sale.
2. The sale must be conducted at the courthouse in the county where the property is located between the hours of 10:00 A.M. and 4:00 P.M. The property will be sold to the highest bidder.

Lenders may seek a deficiency judgment. Borrowers retain the right to redemption for ten days after the sale.

If you decide to file bankruptcy to stop the foreclosure, you can claim a $10,000 homestead exemption. If you hold the property as tenancy by the entirety and only one spouse owes the debt, the property may be exempt from foreclosure.

Question 233: What are the foreclosure and homestead exemption rules specific to North Dakota?

North Dakota lenders may foreclose on a mortgage in default by using the judicial foreclosure process. A court decrees the amount of the borrower's debt and gives him or her a short time to pay. If the borrower doesn't pay within that time, the clerk of the court advertises the property for sale.

In addition, North Dakota requires the lender to give the borrower no less than 30 days' advance notice of its intent to foreclose. This notice must be sent by registered or certified mail no later than 90 days before the suit is filed and must contain a description of the property; the date and amount of the mortgage; the individual amounts due for principal, interest, and taxes due; and a statement that a lawsuit will be filed to foreclose on the property if the amount is not paid within 30 days from the date the notice was mailed. The borrower can stop the foreclosure by paying the delinquent amount, plus foreclosure costs, before the sale is confirmed by the court.

All sales in North Dakota must be made by the sheriff or his or her deputy in the county where the property is located. The property will be sold to the highest bidder, who will be issued a certificate of sale until the borrower's redemption period has ended. Borrowers typically have one year to redeem the property by paying the balance due on the loan plus costs. The time for redemption may be only six months if the mortgage includes short-term redemption rights. Lenders may be able to obtain a deficiency judgment against the borrower in North Dakota.

If you decide to file bankruptcy to stop a foreclosure, you can claim up to an $80,000 homestead exemption.

Question 234: **What are the foreclosure and homestead exemption rules specific to Ohio?**

Ohio lenders may foreclose on a mortgage in default by using the judicial foreclosure process. A court decrees the amount of the borrower's debt and gives him or her a short time to pay. If the borrower doesn't pay in time, the clerk of the court advertises the property for sale.

An appraisal of the property must be made by three disinterested freeholders of the county before the foreclosure sale. A copy of the appraised value must be filed with the court clerk, and the property must be offered for sale at a price of not less than two-thirds of the appraised value.

The notice of sale must be published once a week for three consecutive weeks in a newspaper of general circulation in the county in which the property is located before the foreclosure sale can take place. The sheriff conducts the sale at the courthouse. The property is sold to the highest bidder.

Lenders can obtain a deficiency judgment. The borrower may redeem the property at any time before the court confirms the foreclosure sale by paying the amount of the judgment plus costs and interest.

If you decide to file bankruptcy to stop the foreclosure, you can claim a $5,000 homestead exemption. If the property is held as tenancy by the entirety, the property may be exempt against debts if only one spouse owes the money.

Question 235: **What are the foreclosure and homestead exemption rules specific to Oklahoma?**

Oklahoma lenders may foreclose on deeds of trust or mortgages in default using either a judicial or non-judicial foreclosure process. Using a judicial process, lenders must file a lawsuit to obtain a court order to foreclose. After the court declares a foreclosure, the home is auctioned to the highest bidder.

Unless the borrower waives the right to an appraisal, the property must be appraised before the foreclosure sale, where it must be sold for at least two-thirds of the appraised value. A lender can sue for a deficiency judgment within 90 days after the sale. Borrowers cannot redeem the property once the court confirms the foreclosure sale.

If a power of sale clause exists in the mortgage or deed of trust, a non-judicial foreclosure process likely will be used. Here are the steps for the non-judicial foreclosure process:

1. The lender must send the borrower a written notice of intention to foreclose by power of sale by certified mail at the borrower's last known address. The notice must describe the defaults of the borrower and give the borrower 35 days from the date the notice is sent to cure the problem. If the borrower cures the default in the specified time, the foreclosure can be stopped. If there have been three defaults, then the lender need not send another notice of intent to foreclose and after the fourth default in 24 months, provided proper notice was sent, no further notice is required.
2. The lender must record the notice in the county where the property is located within ten days after the borrower's 35-day notice period has expired. The notice also must be published in a newspaper in the county where the property is located once a day for four consecutive weeks, with the first publishing not less than 30 days before the sale. The notice must state the names of the borrower and lender, describe the property (including the street address) and state the time and place of sale.
3. The property must be sold at public auction to the highest bidder at the time and date specified in the notice. If the highest bidder at the sale is anyone other than the borrower, the winner bidder must pay by cash or certified funds ten percent of the bid amount. If the highest bidder is unable to do so, then the lender may proceed with the sale and accept the next highest bid.

If you choose to file a bankruptcy to stop the foreclosure process, you can claim a homestead exemption of unlimited value as long as the property does not exceed 1 acre in a city, town, or village, or 160 acres elsewhere.

Question 236: **What are the foreclosure and homestead exemption rules specific to Oregon?**

Oregon lenders may foreclose on deeds of trust or mortgages in default using either a judicial or non-judicial foreclosure process. The judicial process involves filing a lawsuit to obtain a court order to foreclose. If the court declares a foreclosure, the home will be auctioned to the highest bidder. The borrower may redeem the property within 180 days after the date of sale by paying the purchase price with interest, the foreclosure costs, and the purchaser's expenses in operating and maintaining the property. If the borrower wants to redeem the property, he or she must file a notice between 2 and 30 days with the sheriff.

If a power of sale clause exists in the mortgage or deed of trust, a non-judicial foreclosure likely will be used. Here are the steps in the non-judicial foreclosure process:

1. The lender records a notice of default in the county where the property is located. The borrower and/or occupant of the property must be served with a copy of the notice at least 120 days before the scheduled foreclosure sale date. The notice also must be published once a week for four successive weeks, with the last notice being published at least 20 days prior to the foreclosure sale. The notice must include a property description; recording information on the trust deed; a description of the default; the sum owing on the loan; the lender's election to sell; and the date, time, and place of sale.
2. The borrower may cure the default at any time before the foreclosure by paying all past due amounts plus costs.

3. The sale must be at auction to the highest bidder for cash. Any person, except the trustee, may bid at the sale.

    The lender cannot obtain a deficiency judgment when a non-judicial foreclosure is used.

If you choose to file bankruptcy to stop a foreclosure, Oregon allows a homestead exemption of up to $25,000 ($33,000 for joint owners). The property cannot exceed one block in a town or city or 160 acres elsewhere. Homestead exemptions also are available for mobile homes or houseboats at reduced amounts.

Question 237: **What are the foreclosure and homestead exemption rules specific to Pennsylvania?**

Pennsylvania lenders must use the judicial foreclosure process to foreclose on a mortgage in default. The process starts when the lender sends a notice of intent to foreclose to the borrower. The notice, which must be sent by first-class mail to the borrower's last known address, cannot be sent until the borrower is at least 60 days behind in his or her mortgage payments. In the notice, the lender must make the borrower aware that his or her mortgage is in default and that the lender intends to accelerate the mortgage payments if the borrower does not cure the default within 30 days, which means that the remaining balance of the original mortgage will come due immediately.

If the borrower does not cure the default by paying, within 30 days, the past-due amount plus any late charges that have accrued, the lender can file suit to obtain a court order to foreclose on the property. If the court finds in favor of the lender, it will issue an order of sale. The property is then sold at a sheriff's sale under the guidelines established by the court. The borrower can cure the default and prevent the sale at any time up to one hour before the sheriff's foreclosure sale.

Lenders have up to six months after the foreclosure sale to file for a deficiency judgment. Borrowers have no rights of redemption once the foreclosure sale is complete.

Pennsylvania does not allow a homestead exemption if you file for bankruptcy to stop the foreclosure, but if the property is held as tenancy by the entirety, it may be exempt against debt owed by only one spouse.

Question 238: **What are the foreclosure and homestead exemption rules specific to Rhode Island?**

Rhode Island lenders may foreclose on mortgages or deeds of trust in default in five different ways: judicial foreclosure, eviction, taking possession of the house, borrower voluntarily giving up possession, or non-judicial foreclosure.

When a judicial foreclosure is used, the lender files a lawsuit to obtain a court order to foreclose. If the court declares a foreclosure, the home will be auctioned to the highest bidder.

If a power of sale clause exists in the mortgage or deed of trust, a non-judicial foreclosure process can be used. The steps include:

1. The lender must mail a written notice to the borrower at his or her last known residence notifying him or her of the time and place of the sale by certified mail, return receipt requested, at least 20 days prior to the first publication of the sale.
2. The lender must publish the sale notice in some public newspaper at least once a week for three successive weeks before the sale, with the first publication being at least 21 days before the day of sale.
3. The notice must include the names of the borrower and lender, the mortgage date, the amount due, a description

of the premises, and the time and place of sale. Any person may bid at the sale, including the lender.

In addition to these two common methods of foreclosure, two special methods are allowed in Rhode Island. One method allows the lender to take possession of the house as long as he or she does so peaceably and in the presence of two witnesses. Witnesses must sign a certificate of possession in the presence of a notary. A second method allows borrowers to voluntarily give up possession of the property in the presence of a notary.

If you decide to file bankruptcy to stop foreclosure, you can claim up to a $200,000 homestead exemption.

Question 239: **What are the foreclosure and homestead exemption rules specific to South Carolina?**

South Carolina lenders must use the judicial foreclosure process to foreclose on a mortgage in default. The lender must file a complaint against the borrower and obtain a decree of sale from a court having jurisdiction in the county where the property is located before foreclosure proceedings can begin. If the court finds the borrower in default, it will give the borrower a set period of time to pay the delinquent amount plus costs. If the borrower fails to pay the amount within the set period of time, the court will order that the property be sold. In most cases this is the process for a foreclosure sale in South Carolina:

1. A notice of sale that includes a description of the property, the time and place of sale, the borrower's name, and the lender's name is posted at the courthouse door and in two other public places at least three weeks prior to the date of sale. In addition the notice must also be published in a newspaper of general circulation within the county where the property is located for the same three weeks.

2. The sale is conducted by the sheriff at the county court-house where the property is located. Foreclosure sales are held on the first Monday in each month between 11:00 A.M. and go until 5:00 P.M.
3. The auction stays open for 30 days after the date of the public sale. During that time, anyone may place a bid higher than the last bid amount and the successful purchaser will be the one with the highest bid at the end of the 30 days.
4. If there is no objection to the sales price of the property within three months of the date of sale, the sale will be considered confirmed and the sheriff will make any necessary deed endorsements.

Lenders in South Carolina may file for a deficiency judgment against the borrower. Borrowers have no rights of redemption.

If you decide to file for bankruptcy to stop the foreclosure process, you can claim a $5,000 homestead exemption.

Question 240: What are the foreclosure and homestead exemption rules specific to South Dakota?

South Dakota lenders can foreclose on mortgages or deeds of trust in default using either a judicial or non-judicial foreclosure process. If a judicial process is used, the lender files a lawsuit to obtain a court order to foreclose. If the court declares a foreclosure, the home is auctioned to the highest bidder.

If a power of sale clause exists in the mortgage or deed of trust, a non-judicial foreclosure process will be used.

If you decide to file for bankruptcy to stop the foreclosure, you can claim a homestead exemption of unlimited value, provided the property does not exceed 1 acre in a town or 160 acres elsewhere.

Question 241: **What are the foreclosure and homestead exemption rules specific to Tennessee?**

Tennessee lenders can foreclose on deeds of trust or mortgages in default using either a judicial or non-judicial foreclosure process. In order to start foreclosure proceedings using the judicial process, the lender must file a complaint against the borrower to obtain a decree of sale from a court that has jurisdiction in the county where the property is located. If the court finds the borrower in default, it will give the borrower a set period of time to pay the delinquent amount plus costs. If the borrower doesn't pay on time, the court orders the property sold.

In most cases, the mortgage or deed of trust includes a power of sale clause, and the non-judicial foreclosure process is used. If you decide to file bankruptcy to stop foreclosure, you can claim a $5,000 homestead exemption ($7,500 for joint owners). Exemptions up to $25,000 are allowed if both spouses are over age 62.

Question 242: **What are the foreclosure and homestead exemption rules specific to Texas?**

Texas lenders can foreclose on deeds of trust or mortgages in default using either a judicial or non-judicial foreclosure process. If a judicial foreclosure process is used, the lender files a lawsuit to obtain a court order to foreclose. If the court declares a foreclosure, the property is sold at auction to the highest bidder.

If a power of sale clause exists in a mortgage or deed of trust, a non-judicial foreclosure sale is used.

If you decide to file bankruptcy to stop foreclosure, you can claim a homestead exemption of unlimited value provided the property doesn't exceed 10 acres in a town, village, or city, or 100 acres elsewhere.

Question 243: What are the foreclosure and homestead exemption rules specific to Utah?

Utah lenders can foreclose on a mortgage in default by using the judicial or non-judicial foreclosure process. To start foreclosure proceedings with the judicial foreclosure process, the lender files a complaint against the borrower and obtains a decree of sale from a court that has jurisdiction in the county where the property is located. If the court finds the borrower in default, it will give him or her a set period of time to pay the delinquent amount plus costs. If the borrower does not pay on time, the court orders the property sold.

If the mortgage or deed of trust contains a power of sale clause, a non-judicial foreclosure is used.

If you decide to file for bankruptcy to stop the foreclosure, you can claim a homestead exemption of $20,000. You must file a homestead declaration.

Question 244: What are the foreclosure and homestead exemption rules specific to Vermont?

Vermont lenders can foreclose on a mortgage or deed of trust in default using either a judicial or non-judicial foreclosure process. Vermont uses a strict foreclosure process. When the borrower is in default, the lender files suit with the court to start the foreclosure process. The borrower will receive a summons to appear in court. If the court rules against the borrower, the lender can take possession of the property or schedule to sell it. For court foreclosures, the borrower usually is given six months from the time of the court ruling to redeem the property. The borrower must pay the full amount stipulated by the court to redeem.

Vermont does not offer a homestead exemption, but if you decide to file bankruptcy to stop foreclosure and you hold the property as tenancy by the entirety, the property may be exempt if debts are owed by only one spouse.

Question 245: **What are the foreclosure and homestead exemption rules specific to Virginia?**

Virginia lenders may foreclose on deeds of trust or mortgages in default using either a judicial or non-judicial foreclosure process. To use the judicial foreclosure process, lenders file a lawsuit to obtain a court order to foreclose. If the court declares a foreclosure, the property will be auctioned to the highest bidder. The borrower has 240 days from the date of the sale to redeem the property by paying the amount for which the property was sold plus 6 percent interest.

If a power of sale clause exists in the mortgage or deed of trust, a non-judicial foreclosure can be used.

If you decide to file bankruptcy to stop a foreclosure, you can claim a homestead exemption up to $5,000.

Question 246: **What are the foreclosure and homestead exemption rules specific to Washington?**

Washington lenders can foreclose on deeds of trust or mortgages in default using either a judicial or non-judicial foreclosure process. If the judicial process is used, the lender files a lawsuit to obtain a court order to foreclose. If the court declares a foreclosure, the property is auctioned to the highest bidder.

If a power of sale clause exists in a mortgage or deed of trust, a non-judicial foreclosure can be used.

If you decide to file for bankruptcy to stop the foreclosure, you can claim a homestead exemption up to $40,000.

Question 247:**What are the foreclosure and homestead exemption rules specific to Washington, D.C.?**

District of Columbia lenders use a non-judicial process to foreclose on mortgages or deeds of trust in default. The terms of sale should be included in the deed of trust, but if they are not established in the deed of trust, the lender must obtain a court order that specifies the terms of the sale.

Before a foreclosure sale can take place, the lender must send a written notice by certified mail, return receipt requested, to the borrower at his last known address. In addition, this notice must also be sent to the mayor of the District of Columbia or his designated agent.

Both notices must be sent at least 30 days prior to the sale, with the 30-day period beginning on the day the notice is received by the mayor. This notice must be given in addition to any notices set forth by the court, the mortgage, or the deed of trust.

Lenders in Washington, D.C., may obtain a deficiency judgment against the borrower for the difference between the foreclosure sale amount and the amount remaining on the original loan. The borrower has no rights of redemption.

If you decide to file for bankruptcy to stop foreclosure, you can claim a homestead exemption for any property that you declare as a residence. If the property is held as tenancy by the entirety, it may be exempt from debts owed by only one spouse.

Question 248: **What are the foreclosure and homestead exemption rules specific to West Virginia?**

West Virginia lenders can foreclose on a deed of trust or mortgage in default using either a judicial or non-judicial foreclosure process. If a judicial foreclosure is used, the lender files a lawsuit to obtain a court order to foreclose. If the court declares a foreclosure, the property is auctioned to the highest bidder.

If a power of sale clause exists in the mortgage or deed of trust, a non-judicial foreclosure can be used.

If you decide to file for bankruptcy to stop the foreclosure, you can claim a homestead exemption up to $25,000.

Question 249: **What are the foreclosure and homestead exemption rules specific to Wisconsin?**

Wisconsin lenders can foreclose on a deed of trust or mortgage in default using either a judicial or non-judicial foreclosure process. If the lender uses a judicial foreclosure, it must file a lawsuit to obtain a court order to foreclose. If the court declares a foreclosure, the property will be auctioned to the highest bidder. No sale may be made for one year from the date the judgment is entered unless the lender waives the right to a deficiency. If the lender waives the right to a deficiency judgment, it only has to wait six months for the sale (two months if the property is abandoned). The borrower can consent to an earlier sale.

If a power of sale clause exists in a mortgage or deed of trust, a non-judicial foreclosure can be used.

If you decide to file for bankruptcy, you can claim a homestead exemption of up to $40,000.

Question 250: **What are the foreclosure and homestead exemption rules specific to Wyoming?**

Wyoming lenders can foreclose on a deed of trust or mortgage in default using either a judicial or non-judicial foreclosure process. If the lender uses a judicial foreclosure, it must file a lawsuit to obtain a court order to foreclose. If the court declares a foreclosure, the property is auctioned to the highest bidder.

If the mortgage or deed of trust includes a power of sale clause, the property can be sold using a non-judicial foreclosure process.

Wyoming does not offer a homestead exemption. If you decide to file for bankruptcy to stop a foreclosure and you hold the property as tenancy by the entirety, the property may be exempt from debts owed by only one spouse.

INDEX OF QUESTIONS

25. What information is included in a foreclosure notice?
26. Will notice of my pending foreclosure be published in the newspaper?
27. What is a loan reinstatement period?
28. What is a mortgage estoppel letter?
29. What must my lender do before foreclosing on or repossessing my home?
30. What is judicial foreclosure?
31. How does the judicial foreclosure process work?
32. What is non-judicial foreclosure?
33. How does the non-judicial foreclosure process work?
34. What is power of sale foreclosure?
35. What is a "no power of sale" foreclosure?
36. How do FHA and DVA foreclosure rules differ from conventional loans?
37. How does the FHA counsel borrowers on the verge of defaulting?
38. What is special forbearance?
39. What is a mortgage modification?
40. What is a partial claim on an FHA mortgage?
41. What is a HUD-approved housing counselor?
42. How does the VA counsel borrowers on the verge of defaulting?
43. What is the borrower's right to reinstate after acceleration?
44. What is a "due on sale" or acceleration clause?
45. What are the acceleration remedies?
46. What is a foreclosure moratorium?
47. What is a deficiency judgment?
48. Can I be evicted from my home?
49. How long does an eviction take?

Chapter 3: **Looking at Liens**

50. What are statutory liens?
51. What are equitable liens?

Chapter 4: **Reporting Your Delinquent Loan**

80. How does a foreclosure impact my ability to buy another home in the future?

Chapter 5: **Stopping Foreclosure Action**

81. What is a foreclosure workout?
82. Should I consider a debt consolidation loan?
83. What is a predatory lender?
84. What is a 125 percent LTV loan?
85. Can I ask for help from family or friends?
86. What is a short pay or short refinance?
87. How can I modify my existing mortgage?
88. How can I set up a repayment plan?
89. Can I give up the property?
90. How do I negotiate a deed-in-lieu of foreclosure?
91. Will the lender accept less than the debt owed on the house?
92. What is a friendly foreclosure?
93. Can I buy back the property after a foreclosure sale?
94. Can I list the property with a real estate agent and delay foreclosure?
95. Can I negotiate to stay in the property even in default?
96. Can I reinstate my rights to the property and stop foreclosure?
97. Can I use a reverse mortgage to keep my home?
98. Will bankruptcy stop foreclosure?

Chapter 6: **Saving Your House with Bankruptcy**

99. What is bankruptcy?
100. How does bankruptcy stop collection efforts and foreclosures?
101. How often can I file a bankruptcy?
102. What is a bankruptcy trustee?
103. What is Chapter 7 bankruptcy?
104. What are the income limits for using Chapter 7?

133. What is an automatic stay?
134. What is my bankruptcy estate?
135. What is community property?
136. What is marital property in a common-law property state?
137. How is property held under a "tenancy by the entirety" handled in bankruptcy?
138. What are property exemptions?
139. What are state exemption systems?
140. How do exemptions work?
141. What are residency requirements for exemption claims?
142. What are federal bankruptcy code exemptions?
143. What are homestead exemptions?
144. Can I get an unlimited homestead exemption?
145. Which states base their exemption on lot size, and how does that work?
146. Which states base their exemption on lot size and equity, and how does that work?
147. Which states base their exemptions on equity only, and how does that work?
148. Which states do not offer any homestead exemptions?
149. What do homestead exemptions protect?
150. What is a declaration of homestead, and what states require it?
151. What is a "wildcard" exemption?
152. How long ago must I have acquired my home to use my state's homestead exemption?
153. What if I bought a new home too recently to use my state's exemption, but I owned a home in the same state previously?
154. What happens to my exemption if I live in the state less than two years?
155. Can my homestead exemption be capped for criminal or deceptive actions?
156. If I don't have any equity in my home, can I keep the home if I file a Chapter 7 bankruptcy?

Chapter 7: **Seeking Help through Credit Counseling**

Chapter 8: **Exploring Foreclosure Sales**

179. What is a public foreclosure auction?
180. What is an "as is" sale?
181. What is the right to redeem?
182. What is the process of appealing a foreclosure sale?
183. What is equity skimming?
184. What is loan loss mitigation?
185. What is a deed-in-lieu of foreclosure?
186. What is a short payoff or pre-foreclosure sale?
187. When will lenders consider a short payoff sale?
188. What is a hardship test?
189. What do lenders consider during the short payoff sale approval process?
190. How does mortgage insurance impact foreclosure sales?
191. What are the tax consequences of a short payoff sale?
192. What are compromise sales?
193. What are the steps to complete a short payoff sale transaction?

Chapter 9: **Special Provisions for Victims of National Disasters**

194. What type of special assistance is available to a homeowner to avoid foreclosure, if I'm a victim of a national disaster?
195. Can I stop foreclosure if I'm eligible for grant assistance?
196. How do I apply for grant assistance?
197. How can I work with my lender to delay foreclosure so I can buy time to apply for a grant or seek other assistance?
198. Can HUD extend foreclosure deadlines for national disaster victims?
199. If I'm in a federally declared disaster area, will my debt problems be reported to credit agencies?

216. What are the foreclosure and homestead exemption rules specific to Kentucky?
217. What are the foreclosure and homestead exemption rules specific to Louisiana?
218. What are the foreclosure and homestead exemption rules specific to Maine?
219. What are the foreclosure and homestead exemption rules specific to Maryland?
220. What are the foreclosure and homestead exemption rules specific to Massachusetts?
221. What are the foreclosure and homestead exemption rules specific to Michigan?
222. What are the foreclosure and homestead exemption rules specific to Minnesota?
223. What are the foreclosure and homestead exemption rules specific to Mississippi?
224. What are the foreclosure and homestead exemption rules specific to Missouri?
225. What are the foreclosure and homestead exemption rules specific to Montana?
226. What are the foreclosure and homestead exemption rules specific to Nebraska?
227. What are the foreclosure and homestead exemption rules specific to Nevada?
228. What are the foreclosure and homestead exemption rules specific to New Hampshire?
229. What are the foreclosure and homestead exemption rules specific to New Jersey?
230. What are the foreclosure and homestead exemption rules specific to New Mexico?
231. What are the foreclosure and homestead exemption rules specific to New York?
232. What are the foreclosure and homestead exemption rules specific to North Carolina?
233. What are the foreclosure and homestead exemption rules specific to North Dakota?

INDEX

ABOUT THE AUTHOR

Lita Epstein, M.B.A., excels at translating complex financial topics critical to people's everyday life. She has more than a dozen books on the market, including *Streetwise® Crash Course MBA, Streetwise® Retirement Planning, Alpha Teach Yourself Retirement Planning in 24 Hours, The Complete Idiot's Guide to Social Security and Medicare,* and *The Complete Idiot's Guide to the Federal Reserve.* She is a faculty member in the College of Graduate Business and Management at the University of Phoenix. Epstein was the content director for the financial services Web site MostChoice.com and manager of the Investing for Women site. She also wrote TipWorld's Mutual Fund Tip of the Day in addition to columns about mutual fund trends for numerous Web sites.